SERVATION

ELOPMENT

and Administration

To

My Affectionate Parents

who are the driving force

behind my academic pursuits

ENVIRONMENTAL CONSERVATION AND SUSTAINABLE DEVELOPMENT

Policy Analysis and Administration

HIMANI

Foreword by

ARUN NIGAVEKAR
(*Chairman, UGC*)

ANAMIKA PUBLISHERS & DISTRIBUTORS (P) LTD.
4697/3, 21A, Ansari Road, Daryaganj
New Delhi 110002
Phones: 3201531, 3281655

First Published 2003

ISBN 81-7975-032-9

PRINTED IN INDIA

Published by Anamika Publishers & Distributors (P) Ltd., 4697/3, 21A, Ansari Road, Daryaganj, New Delhi 110002. Typeset by VGA, MU-61D, Pitampura, Delhi 110088 and Printed at Nagri Printers, Delhi.

Foreword

We are now in the 21st century. This is a century, which is having advantage of the growth and development of science and technology in the 20th century. The 20th century, particularly the latter half, has seen bringing science into use through development of technology. The humans have now become more dependant on materials and material come from our good earth. In a way we have learned to exploit the nature to make our lives more comfortable. Most of our activities require energy in one form or the other. We derive energy from our nature and in the process become the victim of biological imbalances.

This is where the problem of environment conservation comes at the centre stage. It is always difficult to balance environmental conservation and sustainable development. It is a tricky issue, which is linked with the policies and their implementation. It is difficult to make the entire humanity to understand the importance of maintaining of balance ecological system. It is always a fight between the human greediness and the need for understanding the importance of environment for our future generation. It is because of these management of environment has become very important in recent time.

The present book is an attempt to highlight the various aspects and dimensions of environmental problems in India. The author has taken Himachal Pradesh as a base territory to understand the various dimensions of the ecological issues. But what is written is applicable to any other State of India. In fact, it, in a way, addresses the issues connected with environment at the global level.

It is in this respect the book is interesting and much more than that it is useful for researchers that are interested in this very challenging and engaging discipline. I would like to congratulate the author for bringing out a timely publication on a topic, which is of great importance for emerging nation like India.

August 20, 2002 ARUN NIGAVEKAR

Preface

The challenges of environmental management in India are colossal in nature, as compared with the resources available. The need to save the human environment has been felt in the developed world. 'Chipko' movement is one such examples of this need. There is a great need of human attitude towards the environment and the nature at all levels to save this planet.

Man became an active agent in changing the environment to his needs creating an imbalance in ecological situation. Presently the concept of sustainable development is growing momentum for overall well-being of the human beings. The gain in productivity can be sustained only when resources are managed in a way as to permit continuation of socio-economic development in the long run.

Today, we are facing several ecological issues like the population overgrowth, scarcity of space, food, water and other forms of pollution. Environment if affected affects India too much because of population explosion, raw material need, accumulation of waste etc. Environmental pollution is an undeclared bar against mankind and thus needs a serious involvement of environmental administration, through setting 'Environmental Awareness Ethics' and 'Environmental Standards' towards better performance and competence.

The new millennium has already greeted our planet with diverse and convoluted revolutions, innovations and technologies. It is a race against time, however, heartening initiatives have been taken all over the world to tackle the problems of effective management of environmental resources, reducing pollution and strengthening the working ethos of conservation so that sustainability of the life supporting systems on the planet may be ensured and threat to the further minimized.

The problem of pollution and wanton degradation of environmental resources cannot be solved without proper understanding of their causes and effects. Alongside, it is necessary to build up professional capability to develop and adopt policies, measures and programmes for environmental protection.

I wish to express profound gratitude to my husband Dr. Pradeep K. Vaid, Department of Public Administration, ICDEOL, Himachal Pradesh University, Shimla, for his encouragement and constant help throughout the project.

I hardly find words to express my regards and most sincere gratitude to my affectionate parents who have taken deep interest for the accomplishment of this publication.

15th August 2002 HIMANI
Shimla

Contents

1

Introduction

India is facing an acute shortage of Forests and the problem is accentuating every year. Forests have had a vital role in maintaining a balanced ecological system. Forests are among the basic life support system of our planet and are one of the basic physiognomic lives from by which biotic communities may be classified. There is probably no other area of India's environment that has been more viciously attacked and destroyed in the last century the country's forests. Today, India has less than two per cent of the world population. The per capita forest area has decreased from 0.20 hectares in 1981 to 0.11 hectares in 1991, caused by the pressure growing population, urbanization and rapid industrialization. The consequences of this excessive deforestation are increasing flood, soil erosion, heavy siltation of dams build at an enormous expense and change in microclimate. In other words, a progressive depletion of the country's ecological balance during its incessantly towards bankruptcy.

The problem of environment conservation and development has in recent times engaged the attention of various organisations, agencies, and institutions. Men activities have known acquired the potential of artificially due to development of technology, scientific advancement, growth in population and industrialization disturb the delicate balance of biosphere. Introduction of large accounts of pollutants causes serious problems for life on the earth.

Because of these constraints, Himachal State environmental conservation and development policies, plans, programmes and projects are essential to the proper running of the permanent forest estate and ecological balance. The Government of Himachal Pradesh to achieve this purpose is running certain organizations and agencies to ensure environmental conservation and development with the help of machinery for environmental protection in the State like H.P. State Environment Protection and Pollution Control Board, State Council for Science Technology and Environment, and 'HIMURJA' (An Energy Development Agency).

There are a host of human interventions including development activities, which have resulted in considerable environmental degradation. Major human interventions in forests are deforestation, commercial logging, setting-up of protected area, partial closure of forests, etc. which are described as:[1]

- There is increasing deforestation due to commercial exploitation, building of dams, mining and construction activities. Of the world's estimated 8.4 billion hectares of forests in 1990, tropical forests covered 1.76 billion hectares. During 1981-90 tropical forests were lost at the rate of 0.8 per cent (15.4 million ha.) a year, as per estimates of the World Resources Institute. The net annual deforestation during 1981-90 exceeded two per cent in 10 tropical countries of Asia and Africa.
- Commercial logging for industrial activities is increasing rapidly. Eighty-four per cent of such logging took place in closed tropical broad leaf forests in primary (undisturbed forests) during the year 1980. Logging activities is a casual factor for forest degradation and is reflected in rough wood production, which increased by 19 per cent between 1979-81 to 1989-91. Globally, almost 50 per cent of such rough wood is used for industrial purposes, the rest for heating and cooking.
- Setting up of protected areas for conservation purposes has led to complications and conflict-situation with indigenous communities and also denial of many of their rights and privileges.
- Closure of parts of forests for setting up of industries or agro-based activities for private, semi-private land, construction of railways, roads and new settlements has led to

shrinkage to forest cover and increased hardship for local communities in their day-to-day existence.

- Intervention for adhering to international agreements have also alienated many local communities and some of their practices, e.g. tribal hunting of wild animal which goes against biodiversity agreement.
- Policies of economic liberalization, privatization and globalization have both, directly and indirectly, led to reduction of forest cover and cuts in subsidies and grants affecting food subsidies and other welfare schemes.

Objective of Environment Administration

The purpose of Environment Administration is to control the surplus environment pollution by way of neutralizing its effects occurred by a person who himself is required to mitigate the effects of the pollution. Administrative policies, strategies and projects cannot be elaborated or implemented without appropriate instruments. It involves the task of planning, organising, staffing, directing, coordinating, reporting and budgeting. The administrative policy of a government and manner in which the development programmes of environment are likely to be carried out are intimately related. The development of public administration remains an essential prequisite for overall development of environment.

The performance of environment administration depends upon basic seven groups:

(i) Structural or organizational arrangements, roles and relationship;
(ii) Administrative process, procedures and techniques;
(iii) The administrative capability and capacity;
(iv) Systematically planned organized activity;
(v) Classification of objectives and goals;
(vi) Projects must be planned in terms of activities, time and resources; and
(vii) Organizational cultural and values, management styles, leadership and motivated factors.

Edmunds and Lately define environment administration as a concept of "managing human affairs in such a way that biological health, diversity and ecological balance will be preserved."[2]

Administrative structure for forests conservation and development play a vital role in the economy of developing countries like India. A large segment of India's population depends on forests for energy, housing, fodder and small timber. The demands for forest products and services are increasing with the growth in population. The increased demand of forest produce causes of deterioration in forest cover.

The recorded forest area of the country is 76.5 million (about 23 per cent of total area of the country). However, the tree cover is only about 64 million hectare (19.5 per cent of total area) out of which 38.6 million hectares has good forest cover having crown density of more than 40 per cent, 25 million hectares is degraded with crown density in between 10 per cent to 40 per cent. Some forest area is virtually blank, even bereft of any root stock. As per the State of Forest Report, 1995, there is a decrease in the forest cover of 507 sq. kms. in the country as compared with that in 1993. Even the density of good forests is decreased, and the situation is getting worse with further degradation of degraded forests. Table 1.1 provides the picture of forest cover in India:

TABLE 1.1: Forest Cover in India

Year of Assessment	Dense	Degraded	Man groves	Total
1987	357,686	276,583	4,046	642,041
1989	378,470	257,409	4,255	640,134
1991	385,610	250,482	4,242	640,694
1993	385,576	250,275	4,256	640,107
1995	385,756	249,311	4,533	639,600

Source: Forest Survey of India, 1987.

Forest and Environment

Forest has had a vital role in maintaining a balanced ecological system. Forests assist in the essential global recycling of water, oxygen, carbon dioxide and nitrogen. They also influence solar radiation reaching the earth's surface, wind, humidity and temperature, and thus moderate the climate especially the rainfall. The forest maintains the stability of the soil. It holds the soil and the rock together. This prevents landslides.

Forests in the country are subject to very high pressure due to large scale incidents of rural poverty and high population pressure, both human and cattle. Forestry sector needs considerable attention from planners, administrators and politicians in view of the vital role the forests play in the environmental amelioration, and thus improved quality of life. The allocation to forestry sector under successive Five Year Plans and its percentage to the total plan outlay of the country are described in Table 1.2.

TABLE 1.2: Plan Outlay in Forest Sector

Plan	Allocation to Forestry Sector (Rs. in Lakh)	Percentage of Total Outlay
I	764	0.39
II	2,121	0.46
III	4,585	0.53
IV	8,942	0.54
V	20,884	0.51
VI	69,249	0.71
VII	1,85,910	1.03
VIII	4,00,000	1.00

Source: Forest Survey of India, 1987.

The forests of Himachal Pradesh have suffered tremendously over the years from depredation caused by the burgeoning human and cattle population. While snow, wind, insects and pathogens also caused damage to standing trees, it is men who caused the most damage deliberately or inadvertently. Developmental activities have also contributed their share to the disappearances of large areas of forest which were either submerged in the reservoirs of dams, cleared for road construction, or taken for urban expansion. Some of the problems and the factors that influence the management of forests are:

(a) *Fuelwood*

About 90 per cent of the total population of the state is rural and is dependant on forest for meeting their needs of fuelwood for cooking and heating. Annual fuelwood requirement of 8 lakh families living in villages is estimated at 3.2 million tonnes. The manner in which fuelwood is obtained, is also highly damaging. Right holders and the resident population are supposed to collect only dry and fallen wood and twigs, or by lop lower branches of permissible tree species. In practice, even young poles are hacked and trees are badly lopped. This severely impairs the regeneration and protective capacity of the trees and development of a forest. Forests which are in the vicinity of habitations are the most affected.

The greatest pressure is perhaps on the ban oak trees. These are lopped for fuelwood and also for fodder-in the mistaken belief that it is a good feed whereas it comes very low in the ranking of fodder trees. As a result, the areas surrounding villages, give a desolate look and are highly prone to erosion and landslides.

(b) *Grazing in Forests*

Almost 90 per cent of forests of the State, apart from areas taken up for regeneration and plantations, are open to grazing. Cultivation of green fodder in the agricultural fields is virtually non-existent, as are stall-feeding practices. The result is that all forest areas, are open gazed throughout the year. This continuous gazing, without giving any rest, diminishes productivity and gives rise to inferior grasses and bushes like Lantana and Ageratum species.

Migratory grazing creates the intense grazing pressure. There is damage to forests along the routes of migratory grazers. Both Gujjars and the owner of goat flocks, indulge in heavy lopping of trees. Only nominal grazing fee per livestock unit, is charged from migratory graziers.

(c) *Timber Distribution Rights (TD)*

Local people have recorded rights for constructional timber at minimal rates. The ratio between these concessional rates, and market separates is 11:4000 to 5000. Due to the division of families, the number of right-holders is multiplying and the forest have depleted. As marking of the trees, it is not uncommon that some of the best trees are got marked and these may be potential seed bearers. Thus, due to continuous and scientific felling the forests give a look of PBI felled areas with no regeneration.

(d) *Enforcement in Forest Areas*

The menace of encroachment of forest areas is alarming in the undemarcated protected forests, which are without boundary pillars. As these adjoin private lands, they are prone to encroachments. While there is a provision, forest officers do not have any powers under IFA to enter upon any land for survey and demarcation. Government policy to regularize encroachment only encourages encroachers. At present, there are about 7000 encroachment cases, which involved about 17000 hectares of forest area.

According to the survey of India and the National Remote Sensing Agency, of the 19.52 per cent green cover, over 10 per cent are represented by closed forests, over eight per cent farm open forests, 0.12 consists of mangrove forests, and 1.10 per cent comprises coffee plantations. Government has to bring at least 10 million ha of degraded land under forest per annum to achieve ecological balance after a decade.

Another important area of environmental conservation and development is known as "Social Forestry", the objectives of which were spelt out by the National Commission on Agriculture (1976) as:

- (a) firewood supply to replace cow dung,
- (b) small timber supply,
- (c) fodder supply,
- (d) protection of agricultural fields against winds,
- (e) recreational needs.

  Its main components would be:
  - (i) farm forestry,
  - (ii) rural forestry,
  - (iii) urban forestry.

Concept of Environmental Administration

Environmental administration[3] is concerned with the management of human affairs. It seeks ecological balance; equilibrium between man, other species, and the food and energy cycles; minimization of our intrusions on the various ecosystems; maximization of survival of all forms of life. It concerned man himself and how he might continue to live and survive as a creature of earth. As such, the field deals with interaction of human activity with ecology. Man's social and economic wants alter the functions and structure of nature as decisions are made about resource use and waste disposal. With high and rising population densities, with high living standards, industrialized societies, human demands upon resources become so pressing as to be portentous in their effects upon life cycles in the environment.

Environmental Administration, therefore, concerns human decisions, which effects and alter ecological system, and most of these decisions are about man himself, his behaviour, and management of his affairs. In other words, environmental administration is concerned with providing a congruous and workable interface between men's activity and nature. Nature is all the biological process making up the interrelations of organism with their environment. The totality of these interactions between organism, and the environment is referred to as ecology or the ecosystem.[4] Environmental Administration must regulate the demands of men in such a manner that ability of the same environment to sustain his development will remain unimpaired. Good measurement and good administration are closely related. For environmental administration to be effective and systematic, it must consistently, within the existing limitation of knowledge, visualize all processes in total perspective, recognize and understand any process and be able to design, build and operate the management system which would serve as a means to manage any whole. Environmental management employs the following three aspects:[5]

1. ***System Approach:*** A procedure, which recognizes the relationship between natural and non-male system, between system and analysis and management techniques and the

crucial role of the human factor.

2. ***System Analysis:*** A technique of problem formulation, issue definition, and part insight. System analysis concerns itself to finding solutions to a problem and does not concern itself with applying these solutions. It consists of techniques that can be used to find solutions.
3. ***System Management:*** Consists of actual techniques of management for solving problems such as CPM/PERT and others. These techniques prescribe a measurable path to achieve stated environmental correctiveness with milestones along with the way to chart progress.

Role of Administrators

An environmental administrator is a decision-maker whose resource allocation of product design affects ecological life cycles. The most obvious environmental administrators are government decision-makers who control resource use such as, the Department of Environment and Central and State Boards. In state and local governments, these are decision makers who determine water use, air pollution control, land use and energy or transportation franchise. All these governmental officials are environmental administrators in the sense that they decide upon material standards and uses which, upon disposal or recycling, may change the ecological balance. Such governmental officials directly make decisions which characterize them as environmental administrators.[6]

Administrative Structure

Administrative structure represents the policies, methods and processes by which man shapes his environments and control of human action in relation to the environment. For effective and systematic administrative structure towards environmental conservation and development, it must consistently, within the existing limitations of knowledge;

- visualize all process (natural or artificial) in total perspectives;

- recognize and understand any process or problems in the structure and its components, interrelationships;
- be able to manipulate, or otherwise deal with, the interdependences characterizing the process or operation as a whole;[7]

The UN Conference on Human Environment held at Stockholm to which India is a signatory for the protection and preservation of environment provide an inspiration for India to have an administrative structure to implement policies, plans and institutional and financial arrangements for the purpose. The General Assembly of the U.N. also passed a resolution on 15th December 1972 emphasizing co-operation between the states in the field of conservation of human environment. International conference on Environment Education held at New Delhi on 16-20 December 1982, called for massive programme of environment education, research and monitoring World Charter for nature which was adopted by U.N. General Assembly on 28th October 1982 laid down principles of conservation by which all human conduct affecting nature is to be guided and judged. It declared that "nature shall be respected and its essentials shall not be impaired."[8] Conservation of nature should be a part of ending planning.[9] Funds, programmes and administrative structures necessary to achieve the objective of the "conservation of nature shall be provided."

Committee on Environment Planning and Co-ordination

A National Committee on Environment Planning and Co-ordination was constituted in 1972. The committee has been designed for the purpose to act as highest advisory body to the government, and also to work for environment planning. The specific functions of the committee are:

- to do an appraisal of projects from different areas;
- to conduct survey of wetlands;
- to plan for human settlement; and
- to spread environment awareness among the people.[10]

Department of Environment

In 1980, N.D. Tiwari Committee was constituted to recommend some lego-administrative improvements for the protection and preservation of high quality environment for healthy and happy life. The committee submitted its report in September 1980, and made several recommendations. One of the recommendations was for the creation of Department of Environment. Consequently, the Government of India established a separate Department of Environment (DOE) in 1980. It is supporting research on environmental problems and is giving high priority to environment education for creating environmental awareness. At present, the department is headed by a Cabinet Minister. That shows how much significance the government is now giving to it.

The major role of the Department of Environment (DOE) is to act as a "Nodal Agency" for environment protection and growth of balanced eco-system in the country. The specific purpose of the Department is to play a "watchdog role to study and bring to the attention of the government and parliament instances, causes and consequences of environmental degradation of all sectors."[11] Other important functions of the Department are:

- to formulate policy and plan for its implementation,
- to promote research on environmental issues; and
- to maintain liaison with international agencies on environmental problems and other aspects.

The Department of Environment (DOE) functions under the control and supervision of the Cabinet Minister. The Department is assisted and advised by the National Committee on Environment Planning (NCEP) and National Development Board (NDB) at the national level. Other sub-agencies which help and assist the Department to increase its efficiency on technical issues include Botanical Survey of India, which provides data and information about flora of the country and its conservation. Geographical Survey of India helps the Department to develop strategies for the protection of endangered species and conservation of fauna in the country. Central Board of Prevention and Control of Water

Pollution gives advice on matters concerning water pollution and its prevention and control. National Museum of Natural History helps the Department for generating awareness about environment education. The Botanical Survey of India has set up a countrywide network with regional offices. It is also being involved in assessment of environmental impact of development projects. The Zoological Survey of India has been engaged in the survey of Faunal resources and collection of base-line scientific data with regard to their taxonomy, bio-ecology, animal behaviour, pollution etc.

National Environmental Advisory Committee was constituted in 1983. Functions of this committee are:

(i) to identify and highlight the environmental issues;
(ii) to advise on measures for the implementation of environment policy;
(iii) to organize public discussion on national issues of environmental importance;
(iv) to promote public commitment and participation in the implementation of environmental programmes; and
(v) to get feedback on national environmental priorities and plans for the people.

The Departments of Environment, Forest and Wildlife were created under the Ministry of Environment and Forests in 1985. Main functions of the Department include Social Forestry, Farm Forestry, Extension Forestry, Reforestation in degraded forests and research forestry. The Department also maintains and protects sanctuaries of rare species. Other agencies such as National Land-use Development Council, National Wasteland Board and Control Ganga Authority (CGA) were set up in 1985 in the Department of Environment to improve the desert and wasteland. A National Eco-development Board has also been constituted for the socio-economic development by utilizing national resources such as water, soil, plant and animal life.

Further, for higher level administrators, senior executives and planners, a series of carefully structured workshops are organized at the Administrative Staff College of India, Hyderabad, the Indian Institute of Management, Bangalore and the Indian Institute of

Public Administration, New Delhi. Environmental appraisal is an important responsibility assigned to the DOE. This involves evaluation of environment implications and incorporation of necessary safeguards for such activities having a bearing on environment quality. Strengthening active research and training groups in various institutions working areas of interests is necessary. The Ecological Research and Training Centre is one such centre already functioning at the Indian Institute of Science, Bangalore. For the Environmental Information System, Distributed Information Centers were set up at the Industrial Toxicology Research Center, Lucknow, the Central Board for Prevention and Control of Water Pollution, New Delhi and seven other centres of information services in specific subject areas.

Role of Boards

The National Committee on Environmental Planning (NCEP) has constituted Environmental Boards in every State and Union Territory. Under Water Act, 1974 and Air Act, 1981, there is a provision for constituting a common Central Board for prevention of pollution. Under Section 5 of Air Act, State Governments are required to appoint and constitute State Boards for the prevention of pollution. The functions of Central Board for prevention and control of pollution, as mentioned in Section 16(2) of the Air (Prevention and Control of Pollution) Act, 1981, include organising through mass media comprehensive programme regarding the prevention, control or abatement of air pollution. These Boards are empowered to control pollution and provided such power to take immediate action under the Act if by accident or other unforeseen act any poisonous or polluting matter is present in a stream. Further, according to the Water Act, 1974, the Centre and State Governments are to provide adequate funds to the respective Boards for implementation of the objective of the Act.

Environmental Protection Law—The Policy Perspective

Environment law is a newly emerging area or law. Our laws relating to environmental problems are scattered over different statute books.[12] The Parliament has enacted the following legislation to save our environment from being polluted:

(a) The Water (Prevention and Control of Pollution) Act, 1974.
(b) The Water (Prevention and Control of Pollution) Cess Act, 1977.
(c) The Air (Prevention and Control of Pollution) Act, 1981.
(d) The Wildlife (Protection) Act, 1972.
(e) The Forest (Conservation) Act, 1980.
(f) The Environmental (Protection) Act, 1986.

The Environment (Protection) Act, 1986

The Act has been passed by the Parliament of India to give effect to the decisions, taken at the Stockholm Conference in June, 1972 relating to the protection and improvement of environment and prevention of hazards to human beings, other living creatures, plants and property. The Act lays down a comprehensive list of matters with respect to which the central government may exercise full power for the purpose of protecting and improving the quality of the environment.[13]

In 1980, the Tiwari Committee, had also noted some of the major shortcomings in our environmental laws and recommended a comprehensive review and reformation of some central and state laws such as Insecticides Act, 1968, The Water Act 1974 and The Indian Forest Act, 1927.

The committee also highlighted the need for enacting legislation for areas of action left uncovered by the present laws. It further suggested the inclusion of environmental protection in Concurrent list. The Committee, however, regretted that there was no adequate infrastructure for helping the implementing machinery.[14] The areas of environmental concern are:

(a) Environmental Pollution,
(b) Mismanagement of land and water resources,
(c) Depletion of natural resources consciously and in ignorance,

(d) Poor condition of human settlements,
(e) Need for environmental awareness and education.

Plan Approach

In our Five Year Plan the Government of India has squarely admitted the need for environmental administration. However, the country suffers from the absence of a sound National Environment Policy. During the Fourth Five Year Plan (1969-1974) the plan drew attention to the environmental issues in these words, "It is an obligation of each generation to maintain the productive capacity of land, water, air and wildlife in a manner which leaves its successors some choice in the creation of a healthy environment.... Planning for harmonious development recognizes this unity of man and nature. Such appraisal of environmental issues particularly economic and ecological. There are instances in which timely specialized advice on environmental aspects could have helped in project design and the averting subsequent adverse effect on environment, leading to loss of invested resources. It is necessary, therefore, to introduce the environment aspects into our planning and development."[15] The Sixth Five Year Plan (1980-85) attached greater importance to the protection of environment should form a crucial guiding dimensions for planning and development. Environment management has to take note of the impact on health and integrity of our natural resources and, soil, water, forests, wildlife, etc. Of course, the results of poverty of a large section of our population and the means to fulfil the basic utilities of life like food, shelter, clothing and employment have always to be kept in view. But the environment conservation is, in fact, the very basis of all development.[16] This concern for environment is clearly visible in our Seventh Five Year Plan. The plan has accepted Environmental Administration as a major guiding factor for national development. The term Environmental Administration encompassing environments—planning, protection, monitoring, assessment, decision-making, policy formulation and implementation, research and training, education, conservation and suitable use of resources.[17]

Himachal Pradesh came into existence as a State of the Indian

Union on 15th April 1948 as a result of the merger of 30 Punjab Hill States with an area of 28,168 Sq. Kms. The State became a Union Territory in 1956 and continued as such till 19th November, 1966 when the new areas of Kangra, Kullu, Lahaul and Spiti, Shimla, Nalagarh, Una and parts of Dharkalan of Gurdaspur District, were merged with the Pradesh. This increased the area of the State of 55,673 sq. kms. Himachal Pradesh is known for its salubrious climate. It also experiences considerable variation in the distribution of rainfall and temperature due to varying aspects and altitudes. According to the 1981 census, the density of population in Himachal Pradesh was 77 persons per sq. kms. But the pressure on land has increased and according to the 1991 census the density is 93 persons per sq. kms. This is likely to touch 113 persons per sq. kms. By 2001 A.D. The area under forests which was reported as 6,376 sq. kms in 1972-73 had increased to 10,490 sq. kms. by the year 1994-95.

To preserve and protect the forests, the Government of Himachal Pradesh has also framed certain legislative steps to curb the menace of unauthorized fellings and organized timber smuggling. The important legislative enactments are: The Indian Forest Act, 1927, as amended upto 1991 (HP); The Himachal Pradesh Private Forest Act, 1954; Forest (Sale of Timber) Act, 1968; The Wild Life (Protection) Act, 1971; Land Preservation Act, 1978; Forest Conservation Act, 1980; Resin and Resin Products (Regulation of Trade) Act, 1981; Forest Produce (Regulation of the Trade) Act, 1982; Prevention of Specific Corrupt Practices Act, 1983 and Himachal Pradesh Prevention of Forests and Maintenance of Supplies of Essential Commodities Act, 1984.

Management of environment means the proper utilisation, conservation, preservation, control and recycling of the resources for maintaining balanced eco-system. At present very few states have any Environmental Policy of their own. The development vis-à-vis environmental model followed in the States is generally directed by Central policies and laws which do not take into consideration the requirements and unique aspects of different areas. Now time has come to review and reorient these policies and action in unison with environmental perspective of the respective areas before it is too late.

2

Forest Resources and Environment

Earth is the only planet in the universe known to sustain life through its various life-supporting systems like air, water and food resources. However, in recent years these life-supporting systems are gradually declining through the capricious exploitation of earth's resources by the ever expanding human population in order to meet its growing material needs in the name of modernization and development. It is also irony of fate that the poor majority of the world's population is consuming only a fraction of these resources just to keep their body and soul together, while the rich minority of developed countries is over-exploiting these resources in order to maintain their much higher standard of living without regard to the incalculable harm that is being perpetrated to the posterity. Thus, our relationship with biosphere will continue to deteriorate till a new economic order comes into being when the nature's resources will be exploited and utilized in a more rational way to maintain a sustainable development.[18]

Man depends on natural resources from his forest environment for all his basic needs. No doubt, the majority in the industrialized countries is no longer dependent on the natural living resources but the bulk of the rural and section of the urban population in India and the rest of the developing world continue this dependence, especially for their fuel, fodder and timber needs. The forest serves many valuable functions as has been reflected in the national forest policies. Moreover, forest plays an active role as a storehouse of living organisms of potential use and as a regulator of rainfall, soil and water regime, source of many basic needs of the weaker sections of the rural population. The relationship between land, climate and forest is such that if the soil is allowed to deteriorate or lost, degradation of both land and vegetation becomes inevitable. Unfortunately, in the developing countries like India, biotic pressures are intense.

Our Forest

The total area under forests in the world was about 7000 million ha in 1900, by 1975, it was reduced to 2890 million ha. by the 2000 A.D., total global area under forests cannot be more than 2370 million. ha if the present trend of deforestation is not reserved (Khoshoo, 1986).[19] It is rather than ironical that the reduction in forested areas is more pronounced in the tropical belt of the world rather than in the temperate belt. A reduction of 50 per cent is taking place in Asia and the Pacific among the tropical and sub-tropical countries. This is rather ominous keeping in view the explosion of population of humankind and livestock. Coming to India, 90 per cent of the land area was under forests around 3000 B.C. (Warner, 1982).[20] It is believed that hordes of migrants that come to India from treeless countries did not understand the environmental values of forest and denudation of forests continued unabated except during the Mauryan rules. Moghul Emperors converted vast areas of forest land into agriculture land and the British continued the process. During the post-independence period, the destruction and reduction of forest continued for revenue earning, giant hydro-electric projects, road building (especially in mountainous and hilly regions), conversion to agricultural land owing primarily to agriculture-dependent population pressure, providing raw material to forest-based industries, shifting cultivation and hordes of other causes. Currently though the forested area is claimed to 67.22 million ha (22.1 per cent of the total land mass), National Remote Sensing Agency's Photoimergery shows that 13.5 per cent of the total land mass is actually under Forest Cover. The denudation of forest cover in the ecologically sensitive Himalayan region has already begun to exhibit the adverse effect in the form of increasing shortage water, current landslides, increasing incidence of floods, shortage of fuel and leaf fodder, decreased availability of grazing areas. These have compounded the degradation of forest resources and the consequent devastation in addition to over-exploitation of resources by the expanding population of humankind.

The population pressure coupled with accelerated rate of economic growth has widened the gap of demand and supply for forest resources which seems almost unbridgeable. According to a projection (Khoshoo, 1986),[21] in 2000 A.D. demand for firewood, timber, pulpwood will be 2,25,000 Mm^3, 45,700 Mm^3, and 77.70 Mm^3. According to Thapar (1974),[22] the supply position of fuelwood and industrial wood is only 12.5 Mm^3 and 13.5 Mm^3. These require stopping up the present supply by 64 per cent, 110 per cent and 323 per cent under the current low-income growth of the country.

The Problem

The situation is worsening in spite of the lofty aims propagated by three successive National Forest Policies. In India, although the first policy is nearly a century old, the present forest cover is worse than when it was originally proposed. The failure of the national forest policies is perhaps due to their focus on government forests rather than to the land and soil in general. There has been a lack of scientific land-use policy having legal backing and public support. For these reasons, the definition of 'forest' has come to imply land areas constituted as reserve forests and not general tree cover. The tremendous increase in human population, the resultant poverty and the heavy dependence on agriculture have resulted in the use of wood as the main fuel. India's ecology is today no better with the deficit of firewood at 145 million m^3 and 43 million ha of land brought under the plough between 1951 and 1976 for extension of agriculture. The loss of forest area for various purposes during 1951-76 was substantial. About 52 per cent of India's forests are incapable of regeneration largely due to the combined effects of biotic pressure. In a developing country like India, forests have suffered badly because of the failure in land management practices. To what extent the blame can be put up on forest policies? Are the policies wrong or inconsistent or is it that the policies have remained merely documents devoid of the will to implement or people's support?

An analysis of the forest policies of India would reveal the main cause of failure has been, perhaps, viewing forests in isolation rather than taking into consideration the country's soil as a whole.[23]

The Impact of Forest Policies

Policies regarding the management of forests have had a major bearing on the utilization of conservation of biological diversity, especially since a large proportion of India's plant and animal life is intimately connected with forests. Considerable evidence exists of the conservation-orientation of traditional forest dependent communities which, coupled with the absence of technologies that could be employed for large-scale rapid deforestation, ensured that India's forests survived centuries of human use (Gadgil & Guha 1992).[24] Many of these traditions have, however, crumbled being unable to face the onslaught of modern forces of forest destruction.

While popular perception holds the increase in population as being responsible for the beginning of large-scale deforestation in India, environmental historians point out that large-scale forest destruction is rooted in the commercially oriented forest use and ownership policies of the British colonial government, and that such policies have continued in their essence for several years even under post-independence government (Guha 1983 and Tucker 1988).[25] A survey in the mid-1980s revealed that even many national parks and sanctuaries had commercial forestry going on in them (Kothari and others, 1989).[26] Though clear-felling has now been banned, unsustainable logging continues in various parts of India, especially in sensitive areas such as the Northeast.

Conventionally, forest departments in India have prescribed scientific methods of wood harvesting for sustained yields. However, it has been usually impossible to stick to these prescriptions, and even where they were followed, the methods used were not conducive to the maintenance of biological diversity.

In many parts of India, the promotion of a few favoured species has been carried to an extreme through the ironically termed "enrichment plantation", in which a single native species has been encouraged by eliminating other species.

National Forest Policy

A National Forest Policy is essential to the proper running of the permanent forest estate but it needs legal backing and permanent service staffed by competent officers to implement the provisions of the policy. To be effective a forest policy needs be on a national basis with clear perception of specific reasons for maintaining and improving the forests.

India is facing an acute shortage of forests and the problem is accentuating every year. The forests were the natural habitat of wide variety of flora and fauna. Of the total geographical land 11 crore hectares under forests according to the stipulations of the National Forest Policy (1952). As against this requirement, the area classified under forests was only 7.5 crore hectares accounting for nearly 23 per cent of the total geographical area. The first Indian Forest Act was passed in 1865, calling for detailed surveys and classification of forest is reserved and protected. The forest policy of 1984 laid down the broad principles under which forests of different types were to be administered. The Government of India enunciated a new Forest Policy in 1952 which apart from taking other steps, classified forest on a functional basis. The Government received the Indian Forest Act of 1865 with the Act of Forestry.[27]

Forest Policy—Precedence of Agriculture

The first National Forest Policy initiated nearly a century ago, while stressing the important role played by forests in conserving the ecology of the country, had expressed in no uncertain terms that the role of forests was secondary to that of agriculture. However, it suggested that, except for the reserved forests (the preservation of which was essential on climate and physical grounds), if the demand for permanent agriculture arose, forest should give place to it and even in the case of economically rich forests the considerations of forests income were to be subordinate to that of satisfying the needs of the local population for forest produce. Further, the areas excluded from reserved forests should be managed in the interests of the local population for forest produce as distinct from the general public.[28]

Forest Policy—A Perceptible Change

The National Forest Policy of 1952 was framed at time when pressure on land had begun to be exerted and the slogan 'grow more food' was at the cost of forest covered areas. It stressed that a system of balanced and complementary land use was of permanent importance, and contradicted the considerations that neighbouring areas and agricultural requirements should be entitled to a prior and preferential claim over forests.

It supported the necessity of forest not only on the slopes but also in flat areas with dry conditions. It countered demands for the clearance of forests for extension of agriculture, saying that the solution to the food problem of an increasing population lay in intensive cultivation. It suggested that India should aim at maintaining one-third of its land area under forest.[29]

Forest Policy 1988

The current National Forest Policy (1988) recommends increased afforestation view of the wide gap between demand and supply and the evident all round degradation of land. And the desire that the mountainous region should have forests over 66 per cent of the land area. The policy also stresses that the poorer people should be encouraged in the afforestation programmes, and that land grant rules and land ceiling laws should not be subverted. Giving first priority to the local needs, the policy recommends sharing of forest revenues with local communities from social forestry plantations. It is also against the supply of plantations. It is also against the supply of forest raw materials from natural forests to industry, implying mismanagement in the forestry sector, and holding forest-based industries and contractors partly responsible for the deterioration of forests. The only aspects of land-use touched upon are the afforestation of denuded wastelands and the ban on diversion of good agricultural land to forestry plantation. The policy generally refers to pocks legally constituted as reserve forests with no recommendation or restraints on the use of the remaining 77 per cent of the land area outside the reserve forests. There is no suggestion on prohibition of cultivation on steep slopes in Himalayas or the Western Ghats, or in the semi-arid and arid regions. Tree-covered government land not classified as reserve forest continues to be released for cultivation. This includes government land in the mountain belt also. Regularization of encroachment on government land is a priority issue with the Centre and many State Governments. While acknowledging that 29 per cent of all energy consumed in the country is from firewood, compared with 55 per cent from commercial energy, the document has pointed out that the share of forestry sector in the VII plan was around 3 per cent of the commercial energy sector. The afforestation contemplated in the 1988 policy is more in the nature of poverty alleviation schemes rather than through development of forests. While the policy advocated strict grazing practices, entry of cattle into reserve rests continues to be free and unregulated.

Forest and Ecological Balance

Ecology: Ecology in the scientific study of the relationships of living organisms with each other with their environments.[30] It is the science of biological interaction between individuals, populations and communities. Ecology is also the science of eco-systems—the interrelations of biotic communities with their non-living environments. Ecology is directly concerned with environments. It is a natural tool for us insofar as it can provide insight into natural living systems and how they are affected by various kinds of disturbance.[31] The term ecology is derived from the Greek term Oikos, which means "home". The addition of logy, or "study" gives us a term signifying study of home or environment Ecology includes man and all living things, and their interrelations with each other and with the environment. A Standard dictionary describes environment as the aggregate of surrounding things, conditions, or influences. During recent man has been more concerned about his own survival and that of the earth. Thus, ecology has acquired a new broad term—the Environmental Science that focuses greater attention on man and his environment.

Ecology System

Ecological systems are not composed of discrete elements called "structure", and "change", although it was convenient to break them down in this way. More realistically, ecological systems are interacting assemblages in which any two elements affect the third. One element cannot be modifies without changing the other two. Living systems are in dynamic balance with their environments, that is, their structural land dynamic patterns, which are determined by an interaction of environmental forces, which constantly change. Consequently, real systems constantly adapt in response to changing conditions. The principle of ecology that have been developed are most relevant to non-human system because biological limits to behavioral pattern can be shown that is, the organism involved are limited in their capacity for social decision making.[32]

Concepts of Forest Ecology

The forest is one of the basic physiognomic life forms by which biotic communities may be classified. Characterized by the predominance of wood vegetation substantially taller than man, forests are widespread on land surface in humid climates outside of the Polar Regions. The forest may be considered as an assemblage of plants and animal living in a biotic association or biosensors. It is biological comity dominated by trees and other woody vegetation.[33] Ecology is the science of interrelationships of organisms and their complete environment. Forestry ecology, therefore, is concerned with the forest as a biological community, with the interrelationships between the various trees and other organisms constituting the community, and with the interrelationships between these organisms and the physical environment in which they exist.

Sustainable management of sources like forests requires a thorough knowledge of the ecosystem, in particular the role played by the different elements, the intra-system cycles and the exogenous and endogenous changes in them over a period of time. The chief components of a forest eco-system are (a) plants, dominated by trees, forming the primary producers, (b) fauna, forming the consumer element and (c) decomposers, consisting of the micro flora and micro fauna. Tropical Forest Management has seldom been guided by principles of forest ecology. Short-term economic considerations have led to management decision that completely overlook the complexities of the forest eco-system.[34]

Forest and Environment

The influence of forests on environment may be localized or far-reaching. They depend on a number of factors such as situation, climate and type, condition, size and shape of the forest.[35]

(a) *Climate*

The effect of forest on climate is usually localized but it may reach further a field at times. The sun's rays have less effect inside a forest then outside. This effect goes on diminishing as the forest canopy becomes thicker and deeper. Thus, the temperature inside a forest in the tropics is cooler by day than outside. This is also because there is relatively little air movement inside a forest. Its temperature is warmer at night than during the day.

(b) *Rainfall*

Much has been proved and disproved about the effects of forests on rainfall. It seems likely that a combination of factors can cause increase rainfall locally. This can happen when winds pass over large stretches of forest, take up moisture and are then forced upward by hill mass. Such orographic rainfall locally.

(c) *Relative Humidity*

In forest environment the relative humidity is higher than in the open conditions. Within tropical rain forests it may not fall below 80 per cent and indeed, for considerable periods it may be not much less than saturation point. Agricultural crops may benefit from the high relative humidity in a forest environment.

(d) *Wind*

Forest provide protection against the physical violence of winds. They also prevent blowing away of soil. The protective value of trees against strong and desiccating winds and cold winds in temperate climates, and against the hot rays of the sun, brings forestry into close association with agriculture. The shelter effects of trees against wind may be localized but a series of properly sited shelter-belts, oriented more or less at right angles to the damaging winds, can help to ameliorate agricultural conditions.

(e) *Soil*

Due to a complex process forests build up and maintain a forest soil in perpetuity. The agencies which co-operate in this evolution are the physical penetration of the roots in the soil and sub-soil, the physiological process by which a tree receives its raw foods from soil and atmosphere and circulates them within itself, the return to the soil of many of these with the fall of leaves and fruits, and the decomposition of this organic material by the micro-fauna and micro-flora to form hymns. The decomposing agencies work much faster on litter in the tropics than in temperate climates and so there is less evidence of a humus layer in tropical forest soil but the presence of organic matter is shown by darker coloration in the surface layers.

Removal of forest cover may have disastrous results to the soil. In the case of lateritic soil it tends to become hard and unfavourable to free growth. If the removal is for a short period there will be a probably lowering of the fertility. With the return of a forest cover which is maintained for a long time the soil has chance to reconstitute itself.

(f) *Erosion*

When soil is bared long enough to sun, wind and rain it is more than likely that erosion will take place. This destruction of the topsoil is accelerated in tropical conditions by a hot sun and heavy rainfall. The heat of the sun pulverizes the soil, which may be blown away by wind. Any that remains is washed away by the rain because of the likelihood of a great deal of run-off in these conditions and very little seepage. The steeper the slope the quicker is the speed of run-off and loss of soil.

(g) *Drainage*

Drainage prevents absorption of water by roots of the trees and its ultimate transportation into the atmosphere. When an area of forest is clear-felled the water table may rise owing to the absence of the pumping action of the trees. But on the re-establishment of the tree the water table subsides.

(h) *Catchments Area*

The maintenance of forest on catchments areas regulates the flow of water on a slope that run-off in reduced to the maximum. At the same time this can be a precaution against the shilting of reservoirs. But plantation created on level ground may receive rather than give benefits.[36]

The Indian Scenario

Warner (1982), in his studies, has indicated that India had a forest cover of nearly 80 per cent, around 3000 B.C. Waves of migrants came to India and changed the landscape on estimate of the Ministry of Agriculture indicated during mid-eighties the forest cover was around 67.22 m ha i.e. 22.1 per cent of the total land mass, while Centre Forestry Commission (1980) estimated it around 74.8 m ha i.e. 22.7 per cent of the total land mass. According to the last published reports of FSI (1993) the forest cover of the country is 6,40,107 sq. kms., which is 19.47 per cent of the total geographical area of the country. The fourth cycle assessment was indicated that there has been a net increase of 22 sq. kms. Of forest cover since the third cycle assessment. Actual forest cover by density class and comparative situation of the same during 1991 and 1993, as published by the Ministry of Environment and Forests (1990-95) are presented in Table 2.1.

TABLE 2.1: Actual Forest Cover by Density Class and Comparative Situation

Recorded Forest (77008 M ha)		Actual Vegetation (64.0107 M ha)	
Un-classed Forest	12.208%	Open Vegetation	25.025%
Protected Forest	23.308%	Dense Vegetation	38.5576%
Reserved Forest	41.492%	Mangrove Vegetation	0.4256%

Source: Ministry of Environment and Forests.

The Indian strategy towards conservation of Forest resources, move around creating conservation, limited production and production forests. The Forest (Conservation) Act, 1980 is being implemented. The enactment of this Act, according to the governmental sources, has brought down the rate of diversion of forest land to non-forest land from 1,43,00,000 ha to 25,000 ha per annum.

Participatory Forest Management has been the focal point of the National Forest Policy, 1988, in which efforts have been made to achieve the desired goals like forest conservation, extension of tree cover and fulfilment of the fuel requirement of the people. NFAP (National Forestry Action Programme) has been made operational with the assistance of UNDP since 1993 and initially areas like resource economics, forest industries planning, institution development and forest sector review, have been taken care of. Efforts have also been made to devise effective methods to control forest fires and various schemes are running in eleven states.[37]

Exploitation of Forests

There was a time when forests covered a much larger area of the land surface than they do now. Their partial or complete destruction has been brought about by a variety of reasons but in many cases the primary cause has been man's desire to clear an area in order to grow foodstuffs. Cultivation may have taken place for a short period, after which the farm was abandoned and in due course tree growth would be likely to return on a small-scale farming and to permanent clearing for habitation. As time when on, the once so-called inexhaustible forests dwindled both in quantity and quality to such an extent that it proved to be inadequate for the nation's needs, both instantaneous and ecological.[38]

There is probably no other area of India's environment that has been more viciously attacked and destroyed in the last century than the country's forests. According to official statistics India lost between the period 1951-1972, 3.4 million hectares of forest lands to dams, new crop lands, roads and industries, meaning thereby an annual rate of deforestation of about 0.15 m. hectares. Though Government Statistics point out that the approximately 23 per cent of the country's total area, that is, 75 million hectare, is classified as forest lands. But this leads to be a misleading statement. It simply means that this vast area is under the control of forest departments. There, however, is no guarantee that it has tree cover. A report of the National Committee on Environment Planning also clearly states that no more than 12 per cent of the country's total land surface is under adequate tree cover.[39]

Table 2.2 indicates the extent of the forests lost for various logical or illogical reasons during the period 1952-72.

TABLE 2.2: Forest Area Lost in India During the Period 1952-72

Purpose	Area (in thousand hectares)
1. River Valley Projects	401
2. Agricultural Purpose	2,433
3. Roads and Communications	55
4. Establishment of Industries	125
5. Miscellaneous	388
Total Area Lost	3,402

(This represents an average annual loss of 1,55,000)
Source: Forest resources of tropical Asia, FAO, 1981.

As it is clear from the above table that the forest area lost during the last two decades for various reasons has been quite significant though comprehensive figures for reclaiming the losses or compensating the forest loss by some alternative afforestation or conservation measures are not readily available but from all round apprehensions expressed about fast receding forest cover in country indicates the failure or absence of reasonable success of such measures.

A 1981 FAO report on Forest Resources of Tropic Asia clearly warns that the region is faced with serious decrease in its forest stock. "There is no evidence to predict that the great variety of forest services and functions, such as harbouring of wild life, stabilization of soil and of water can be re-established in the foreseeable future", says the report. The consequences of this excessive deforestation are increasing floods, soil erosion, heavy siltation of dams built at an enormous expense and changes in microclimate. In other words, a progressive depletion of the county's ecological balance, driving the incessantly towards bankruptcy.

Strategy for Forestry

Considering the continental dimension of problems, it is difficult to prescribe a universal strategy. However, fundamental objectives should be clearly stated and flexibility should be built into take into account specific regional and local problems. Prescribing the objectives of forestry depends on how one defines development and values judgements are inescapable. Taking into account the problems generated by past approach, an alternative has to aim at:

(a) ecological restoration of degraded and denuded areas, and
(b) redirecting resources use to ensure the fulfilment of basic needs of the peoples giving almost priority to those of the neediest.[40]

Reorienting Forestry to achieve the above objectives are discussed below.

1. *Land-use Policy*

A Forest Policy, however well conceived, could face serious problems at the implementation stage it is not likely with the policies in sector like agriculture, industry and energy. This has been one of the most drawbacks of the 1952 National Forest Policy. Most of the land-use conflicts can be attributed to the divergent objectives pursued by different sectors. To overcome this a comprehensive land-use policy has to be formulated stipulating the basic principles guiding the allocation of land for different purposes. Land-use should be strictly guided by a capacity classification so that deterioration from issue is prevented.[41]

A sound forest forms a component of the land-use policy and broadly indicates the priorities in the sector. Since forests have multiple uses, some of which are partially incompatible, guidelines for trade-offs have to be prescribed. When uses are totally incompatible, zoning can be restored to. Unless the primary function of an area is clearly prescribed, the possibility of diverting it for less important uses is quite high. A functional zoning which will help to meet the broad objectives of forest resources management is indicated below.[42]

(a) *Protection Zone*

Most of such regions which are susceptible to serve erosion can be included in this zone. The primary objectives of management are to ensure ecological stability through watershed protection, conservation of genetic diversity and protection of wildlife and wilderness values. Low intensity recreation often affects on primary function of the area.

(b) *Production Zone*

This zone consists of all areas, which are intensively managed for wood production particularly to meet the industrial and urban demands. Extensive wastelands available in the country have to be included in this zone and taken up in a phased programme.

(c) *Village Zone*

A village zone is identified and managed with the social objective of meeting basic needs, particularly timber, fuelwood, fodder and green manure. A major part of the raw material requirements of small-scale industries are also to be from this zone.

2. *Institutional Framework*

Failure in implementing a policy mostly arises from institutional constraints. The emphasis, has to create appropriate institutions, which enable beneficiaries to have a decisive say in forest management. Benefits from the protection zone largely occur to society as a whole, and hence protecting the area has to be under public sector control. The forest department can fulfil this role effectively. Since the objective management of production zone is to achieve industrial wood supply, industries could also be directly involved in raising and managing plantations. One approach would be lent out a sufficient extent of land to industries so that production of wood is integrated. This is not only likely to reduce the burden of the government, but also help in more efficient utilization of land than today.[43]

3. *Legal Safeguards*

Policy legislation and creation of appropriate institutions are in themselves inadequate to ensure that resources are managed scientifically. A comprehensive legislation form the cutting edge of public policy. The existing Forest Act formulated in 1927 has very limited objectives of keeping away people from Forests. Although the National Commission on Agriculture emphasized the need for development-oriented legislation, the outcome, namely the 1980 Forest Bills has only made the punitive provisions of the forest Act more draconian. There are two approaches to provide legal safeguards for ensuring the implementation of a forest policy. Forest Legislation can form part of a comprehensive natural resources management Act or alternatively environmental safeguard can be incorporated into Forest Acts and Rules. Some of the essential components of a forest law are as follows:[44]

(a) Activities that are permitted, not permitted, should be clearly defined for zone separately. This should be applicable not only to the public but also to the agencies entrusted with the management of forests in different zones. At present no legal provision exists to curb mismanagement of forests.

(b) Agencies concerned with the management of forest should prepare a long-term management plan and this should contain a detailed statement of the expected environmental impacts.

(c) A comprehensive legislation should contain provisions that enable an individual or group to see the intervention of the judiciary for acts of omission on the part of those responsible for management.

Forests in Himachal Pradesh: An Overview

Himachal Pradesh, as the name implies, lies in the lap of Himalayas and extends from the perpetual snowy mountains separating it from Tibet down to Punjab plains. It lies between 30°-22'-44" and 33°-1'-40" north latitudes and 75°-45'-55" and 79°-04'-20" east longitudes.[45] The evaluation varies from 244 m in the foothills to 6,579 m. Such as wide range in altitude results in marked difference in the climatic conditions met within different parts of the state. The hills above 4,500 m remain almost always under snow.

For hill states like Himachal Pradesh, where the forests have to protect hillsides against erosion, moderate the water flow and ameliorate physical and chemical factors of the locality, the National Forest Policy lays down that forests should cover two-thirds of the geographical area. As per the legal definition of the term 'forest', forest cover should be 37,591 sq. kms. or 67.52 per cent of the total geographical area of Himachal Pradesh. But in reality the well-wooded area with a good density is much less. Nearly 16,376 sq. kms. or 29.41 per cent of the so-called forest area is under Alpine pastures and perpetual snow cover. This leaves only 21,215 sq. kms. or 38.11 per cent of the geographical area under forest covers of some sorts. However, satellite imagery places the forest cover of the state at 12,501 sq. kms. only or 22.4 per cent of the geographical area. This is far below the stipulated norm of 66 per cent required for hill states. Thus, a majority of the forest area is either under rocked, rocky or blank.[46]

The economy of the state and that of the people also closely depends upon the forests. The villagers in Himachal Pradesh depend upon forest for their day-to-day needs, such as cattle grazing, firewood, timber for agricultural implements and construction. The horticulturists depend upon forests for the supply of trees for the manufacture of packing cases. Industrialists also depend upon the raw material for a number of wood-based industries. Local population also derives some income from the collection and sale of medicinal herbs. They also get employment in forests, working on plantations and nurseries during their spare time. Forests are of vital importance to conserve water and soil to reduce the silt load in the dams constructed on various rivers, and to make continuous flow of water possible in order to meet the requirements of electric generation. The nature's wonderful heritage in the form of wildlife depends on conservation of forests.

Table 2.3 provide an idea of distribution of forests by crown density in Himachal Pradesh:

TABLE 2.3: Distribution of Forests by Crown Density (FSI 1995)

1.	Forest area (legally defined	3,759 sq. km.
2.	Area under tree cover	2,501 sq. km.
3.	Dense Forest (Crown density above 40 per cent)	9,565 sq. km.
4.	Open Forest (Crown density to 1-40 per cent)	2,936 sq. km.
5.	Scrub Forest (Crown density below 10 per cent)	1,845 Sq. km.

As it is clear from the above table that the forest area already legally defined in Himachal Pradesh is 37,591 sq. kms, whereas the area under tree cover and dense forest area is 12,501 sq. km. And 9,565 sq. kms have comprehensive figures. As per legal classifications of the State has been categorized into Reserve Forest, Demarcated Protected Forest, Undemarcated Forest and Unclassed. The extent of Forest area under each category is presented in Table 2.4.

Only the 12,254 sq. km. falling into reserve forest and demarcated protected forest category have been demarcated on the ground and the rest of the area is yet to be demarcated with

TABLE 2.4: Classification of Forest in H.P.

1.	Reserve Forest (RF)	1,896 sq. km.
2.	Demarcated Protected Forest (DPF)	10,358 sq. km.
3.	Undemarcated Protected Forest	22,991 sq. km.
4.	Unclassed Forest	868 sq. km.
5.	Other—like Cantonment and Municipal Forest	1,478 sq. km.
	Total	37,591 sq. km.

Source: Department of Forests, Government of H.P.

boundary pillars. Apart from demarcating the forest, its entry in the revenue record is also important. Only 9244 sq. km. (24.6 %) of the forest area out of the total forest area stands entered into the revenue records. This situation has created problems regarding forest protection. Serious damage has been caused to the forest wealth by way of encroachments, illegal felling of trees and breaking of land for quarrying and mining. This leads to prolonged litigation in many cases. While for the purposes of survey and demarcation, four divisions have been created and each is headed by a collector of forests, the work has not progressed with desired speed. Instructions have also been issued by the Government to enter all forest areas on the basis of forest records into revenue record. This is yet to be implemented in many districts.

On the face-value Himachal Pradesh seems to be comparatively in a happier position in the context of national averages. Table 2.5 gives an idea of the area under forests in Himachal Pradesh and at the National level. The per cent forests coverage has also been juxtaposed. Similarly, for the population figures in Himachal Pradesh and in the country as a whole per capita forest area has been worked out and compared.

Against the national average of 22.73 per cent of the area under forests in the country Himachal Pradesh can boast of 38.00 per cent. Similarly against per capita forest area in the National average of 0.11 (thousand hectares), Himachal Pradesh has better figures of 0.5 (thousand hectares) per person. But a deeper thought makes this position not so comfortable. Himachal Pradesh consists of hilly terrain criss-crossed by big and small rivers, rivulets, nallas, glacier and deep gorges. There is apprehension of erosion

TABLE 2.5: Comparative Studies of Forest Resources

Area '000 Ha. and Population '000 No.

Geographical Area	Forest Area	Percentage of forest to geographical area	Population 1981 census	Per capita forest area
Himachal Pradesh 5,5567	2,114	38.00	4,238	0.50
India 3,28,779	74,723	22.73	6,81,268	0.11

Source: India's Forest 1980, Issued by Central Forestry Commission, Government of India.

every time everywhere whenever extremities of weather strikes. The one-third of the State is snow-bound making any vegetation on that area impossible. Being a State saddled with the responsibility of sitting a large number of irrigation and hydroelectric dams Himachal Pradesh needs a bigger forest cover for their conservation. Similarly, roads are life-line for a hilly area, being the only transport measure possible, which again is a bigger drain on ecological balance. Thus, the better figures for Himachal Pradesh are no consolation. These are rather the danger signals to improve the condition and bring the forest ratio to stipulated 50 per cent of total geographical area without any further loss of time.

The forests of Himachal Pradesh are important for the country from ecological point of view. They form the upper catchments areas of the rivers in Northern India. After the opening up of the region by way of roads and paths the hitherto inaccessible and valuable forests became accessible. At the same time, due to the increase in population and consequent urbanization the demand for timber and other forest produce went upto the unimaginable extent. Suddenly, the forests, which were perceived as intangible wealth, became a tangible source of income. Table 2.6 gives an idea of Forest distribution in the State.

Table 2.6 shows that some of the districts, particularly those of Chamba, Kullu, Mandi and Shimla are well forested, whereas other districts like Lahaul and Spiti, Kinnaur, Bilaspur have a low coverage. Resultantly, the timber and fuelwood to be moved over long distances to meet the domestic requirements of local people.

TABLE 2.6: Forest Distribution in the State

District	Geographical Area	Legally Classified	Actual		Total	%age of Geographical Area
			Dense	Open		
Bilaspur	1,167	427	101	65	166	14.22
Chamba	6,528	4,891	1,625	392	2,017	30.90
Hamirpur	1,118	249	156	60	216	19.30
Kangra	5,739	2,794	808	625	1,433	24.98
Kinnaur	6,401	6,408	56.5	68	633	9.88
Kullu	5,503	4,914	1,817	131	1,948	35.39
Lahaul & Spiti	13,835	9,371	–	17	17	0.12
Mandi	3,950	2,078	839	462	1,301	32.95
Shimla	5,132	3,447	1,921	299	2,220	43.26
Sirmour	2,825	1,723	740	279	1,019	36.05
Solan	1,936	732	164	251	415	21.46
Una	1,550	557	175	220	395	25.66
Total	55,673	37,591	8,911	2869	11780	21.16

Source: State of Environment Report, Himachal Pradesh, March, 2000.

Forests are not uniformly distributed in the State and are mostly confined to the higher hills and interior valleys, and have inadequate road communications. Most of the forests are state owned, and private forests are small in extent. But even this has posed problems of protection, as boundaries between private and government forest are not well defined. Table 2.7 depicts an idea about the Altitudinal Zonation of Forests in Himachal Pradesh in view of classification and flora of the State.

More than 95 per cent of the species are endemic to Himachal Pradesh and are characteristic of Western Himalayan flora. About 5 per cent (150 species) are exotic and have been introduced over the last 150 years. The enumeration of different plant species in the state are as following:

1. Flowering plants	3,120 species
2. Conifers	12 species
3. Pteridophytes	124 species
4. Orchids	38 species

Source: State of Environment Report, Himachal Pradesh, March 2000.

TABLE 2.7: Altitudinal Zonation of Forests

Classification based on Altitudinal Zones	Flora of Himachal Pradesh	
1. Lower Mountain Zone (up to 1,000 m above ms l	(a) Trees:	Mhair, Siris, Kachnar, Semal, Tun, Mango, Behul, Shisham, Ritha, Tut, Bahera and Chil
	(b) Shrubs:	Vitex, Munj, Ber, Dodonea, Bamboo
	(c) Grasses:	Vetiver, Sanchrus, Munj
2. Middle Mountain Zone (up to 1,000-2,000 m above ms l)	(a) Trees:	Kunish, Poplar, Willow, Ohi, Robina, Drck, Kail, Chil, Toon, Behmi, Chulli, Walnut, Khirik
	(b) Shrubs:	Vitex, Berberis, Carrisa
	(c) Grasses:	Lolium, Dactylis, Phelum, Phylaris
3. Temperate Zone (from 2,000-3,000 m above ms l)	(a) Trees:	Deodar, Fir, Spruce, Maple, Ash, Bhoj Patra, Horse-Chesnut, Alder, Robinia, Poplar, Walnut
	(b) Shrubs:	Beberis
	(c) Grasses:	Festuca, Dacylis, Bromus, Lucrene, Whit, Clover, Red, Clover, Dioscorea
4. Alpine Zone (above 3000 m above ms l)	(a) Trees:	Birch, Juniper, Cypress, Willow
	(b) Shrubs:	Saussurea Lappa, Cotoneaster, Microphylla, Artemesia
	(c) Grasses:	Festuca, Arundinacea, Dectylis Glomrata

Source: State of Environment Report, Himachal Pradesh, March, 2000.

Himachal State Forest Policies: An Observation

The industrial framework for the administration of forest lands and resources in Himachal Pradesh dates back to the 19th century when forest settlements were carried out. These legal settlements were made at the end of the 19th century and in the first two decades of the 20th century. These still provide the basic institutional framework for administering forest resources. However, the State over a period of time has regulated public access to Government lands and forests—principally through the Revenue and Forest Departments.

The Forest settlements accepted and formalized the rights of the local people. Although, in this period there have been many new laws, rules and regulations affecting the use of forest resources, remain unchanged—except that the number of people holding them, has increased significantly. Today, the demands made on forest resources through honouring of these rights have increased enormously. Similarly, the institutional and legal environment in which this historical legacy is implemented has become exceedingly complex and complicated. It is felt that coupled with a need to create public awareness, certain legislative measures are also required to preserve and protect forest resources—and to serve as a deterrents for unscrupulous elements.

The Government of Himachal Pradesh from time to time has strengthened the legislation through the enactment of various Acts and Rules. These legislative and administrative steps were considered necessary to curb the menace of unauthorized removals and of organized timber smuggling. As a result, forests offences are now are of a petty nature. The system of the contractor agency—which was fraught with the menace of illicit felling and timber smuggling, has been done away with by completely nationalizing forest harvesting and resin tapping, and entrusting it to the H.P. State Forest Corporation.

The legal provision on control, use and management of forests, have developed over a period of time. These are scattered over several acts, rules and settlement reports, notifications and Government orders. At different times, legal instruments were introduced to deal with administrative exigencies. As a result, the legislation and laws are not a coherent body of provisions, but are a contradictory body of conflicting objectives, modalities and provisions.

While, the Indian Forest Act of 1927, remains an all pervasive Act for the constitution, management and protection of forests, various other laws, acts and rules enacted by the State of Himachal Pradesh and having bearing as under:[47]

1. *Himachal Pradesh River Rules, 1971*

These rules have been made to regulate the transit of timber on the rivers of the state. For landing, floating or rafting timber in any river, the permission of Divisional Forest Officer is required.

2. *Forest Produce Transit (Land Routes) Rules, 1978*

These rules were made to regulate the movement of forest produce by land routes into, from and within the territorial limits of the State.

3. *Mandi and Chamba Minor Forest Produce Extraction and Export Act, 1937*

These Acts regulate the collection of herbs and their export.

4. *Wildlife (Protection) Act, 1972 as Amended in 1990*

This deals with the setting up of Protected Area, National Parks and Sanctuaries and the regulation of activities in these areas for the protection of both flora and fauna.

5. *Himachal Pradesh Land Preservation Act, 1978*

In view of the hill terrain of the State, the felling and sale of trees in private areas is regulated under a 10 year felling programme. Notwithstanding the provision, lots of damage was done to the Government forests under the garb of private area felling. This was a result of ill-defined boundaries between Government forests and private lands.

6. *Himachal Pradesh Forests Produce (Regulation of Trade) Act, 1994*

Under this Act, the forest working in private areas has been nationalized and this is to be done only through the H.P. State Forest Corporation.

7. *The Himachal Pradesh Resin and Resin Products (Regulation of Trade) Act, 1981 and the Rules made hereunder*

Under this Act, the trade in resin from private areas has been nationalized and resin has to be sold only to the H.P. State Forest Corporation.

8. *The Forest Conservation Act, 1970 as Amended in 1988*

This Central Act provides that no forest land can be transferred for non-forestry uses without the prior approval of the Government of India. It also provides for punishments to offenders and to those abet offence. This Act has acted as a deterrent against liberal transfer of forest lands for so-called development purposes.

9. *Indian Forest (H.P. Second Amendment) Act, 1911*

This Act has assumed considerable importance as forest officers are now empowered to confiscate vehicles involved is an offence.

State Forest Policy

To give proper orientation to the management of forests, increasing the tree growth and forest areas within the ambit of National Forest Policy, a new dynamic State Forest Policy has been framed and approved by the Government during Sept. 1980 on the guidelines laid down by the late Prime Minister of India Mrs. Indira Gandhi, in her letter of April 1980 addressed to all the Chief Ministers of India. According to Himachal Government, Himachal is one of the foremost states in India to adopt such a progressive policy within the framework of National Forest Policy which is the need of the hour in India. Keeping in view the various compulsions of land uses the State of the geographical area under real wooded forestry by the year 2000 A.D.[48]

Salient Features of the State Forest Policy

1. The Forest Policy is to become an integral part of the land management policy. The policy is to consider the available land resources and earmarking them to meet and balance the conflicting demands of different segments of society land.
2. Transfer of all areas acquired by the Government under the Land Ceiling Act, 1972, and the Village Common Lands Act, 1974, bearing forest crops or having a potential

for being brought under tree cover, to the Forest Department within a year.

3. Crash afforestation programme are to be formulated to increase the area under plantation and increase the density of forest cover in areas already notified as forest over the next 20 years i.e. by the year 2000.
4. Felling is to be carried out strictly in accordance with the prescription of the sanctioned working plans. All felling including those for meeting the requirements of right holder and for packing cases—are to be accounted for against the prescribed yield. Fresh felling will be permitted only when regeneration of the areas felled, has been secured.
5. Demarcation of all un-demarcated and un-classed forests, and the completion of settlements within 10 years.
6. Rationalization of timber distribution rights for bona fide domestic use. The right-holder rate to be placed on a sliding scale, with higher rates for those better placed. Timber for new houses to be given once in life time only and for repairs, this will be once in 10 years.
7. Alienation of forest lands for agriculture in the shape of Nautors to cease.
8. Master plans for management of watersheds.
9. Strengthening of the wildlife wing.
10. Forestry programmes to meet requirements of the people and encourage people's participation.
11. Fuel saving devices to be encouraged.
12. Strengthening of Indian Forest Act to stop unauthorized removals and transport of timber.
13. Stoppage of all hidden subsidies, which affects revenue from forests.
14. Formulating programmes for cattle and pasture improvements checks incidence of forest grazing.
15. Nationalization of sale of trees from private lands.
16. Encouragement of eco-tourism.
17. Setting up of an effective monitoring and evaluation unit within the forest department.
18. Creation of facilities for carrying out applied forestry research.

Some Aspects of Raising Plantation in H.P.

Keeping in view ensuring environmental stability and maintenance of ecological balance including atmosphere equilibrium which are vital for sustenance of all life forms, human, animals and plants—Himachal Pradesh State Forest Policy is meeting the requirements necessary to maintenance of environmental stability through new plantation of various categories and species of tree.

New plantation of trees in classified forest in a good measure in assessing the extent and rate of afforestation. The figures provided in Table 2.8 with regard to the new plantation of various varieties of trees in Himachal Forest during the period 1961-84 are reasonably impressive. There is a steady increase in covered

TABLE 2.8: Forest Plantation in Himachal During 1961-1984

(Area in Ha.)

Name of species	Area planted from 1961-62 to 1981-82	Plantation raised during 1982-83	1983-84	Total area manmade Forest up to 31.3.1984
1. Deodar	42,950	3,865	2,286	49,101
2. Kail	5,054	294	394	5,702
3. Fir/Spruce	8,869	280	246	9,395
4. Chil	1,18,614	8,487	9,896	1,36,997
5. Other coniferous	108	–	–	108
6. Walnut	1,738	83	64	1,885
7. Willow	1,838	332	286	2,456
8. Mapple	53	40	–	93
9. Khair	63,118	6,275	5,632	75,025
10. Shisham	2,756	197	262	3,215
11. Bamboo	1,138	55	60	1,253
12. Mulbery	1,268	4	–	1,272
13. Poplar	1,399	395	295	2,089
14. Kobina	4,965	765	550	6,280
15. Leucalna Eucalyptus	-	641	–	641
16. Other broad leaved species	17,115	–	–	17,115
17.	33,235	5,134	4,699	43,070
Total	3,04,220	26,807	24,672	3,55,697

Source: Himachal Pradesh Forest Statistics, 1982, Department of Forest Environmental Conservation, Himachal Pradesh, Shimla.

area year after year. Coniferous trees, such as Deodar, Chil in higher hills, and Khair and Eucalyptus in the lower areas dominate the plantation. Eucalyptus plantation seems to have been discontinued after 1982, evidently, a wise policy. But keeping in view the ambitious goal of 50 per cent forest cover in the State Forest Policy, this modest annual rate may not be much helpful in the realization of targeted percentage. The following table gives an overview of new plantation of various categories during the period 1961-1984.

Forests, though as per legal definition form 67 per cent of the total geographical area in Himachal Pradesh, but really wooded is much less. As per Forests Survey of India Report, 1989, the forest area in the State with more than 40 per cent tree density is only 8911 sq. kms, the balance area is poorly stocked, degraded has a crown density below 40 per cent. Moreover, the culturable forest area is only 21,315 sq. kms and the balance 16,276 sq. kms is under Alpine pastures and permanent snow, etc. The Forest Policy for H.P.

TABLE 2.9: Area Planted upto 1992-93

(Area in Ha.)

Name of Species	Area planted up to 1992-93
1. Deodar	77,100
2. Kail	8,800
3. Fir/Spruce	13,400
4. Chil	2,18,000
5. Other Conifers	100
6. Walnut	2,600
7. Willow	4900
8. Khair	1,21,2000
9. Shisham	7,800
10. Bamboo	2,200
11. Mulbery	1,300
12. Poplar	8,100
13. Robinia	25,700
14. Other Broad Leaves Species	1,38,300
Total	6,29,500

Source: Department of Forest, Government of H.P.

formulated in the year 1980 lays down that the year 2000 A.D., the forest cover having adequate stocking in the State should be increased to 50 per cent. Intensive afforestation activities on the Government wastelands, undemarcated protected forests and demarcated protected forests is the only way to achieve the above targets. Total plantation of different species raised in the State upto 1992-93 and 1993-94 to 1995-96 are given in Tables 2.9 and 2.10.

TABLE 2.10: Area Planted from 1993-94 to 1995-96

Name of species	Plantation raised during			Total area planted 1961-62 to
	1993-94	1994-95	1995-96	1995-96
1. Deodar	3,154	3,360	3,918	87,532
2. Kail	328	354	613	10,095
3. Fir/Spruce	761	412	445	15,018
4. Chil	8,088	9,813	8,025	2,43,926
5. Other conf.	–	–	–	100
6. Walnut	13	31	38	2,682
7. Willow	486	837	585	6,808
8. Khair	4,697	4,941	3,770	1,34,208
9. Shisham	296	533	971	9,600
10. Bamboo	91	85	361	2,737
11. Mulbery	–	–	–	1,300
12. Poplar	485	578	619	9,782
13. Robina	2,526	2,334	2,226	32,786
14. Other broad leaved species	6,880	7408	8,658	1,61,246
Total	27,805	30,686	30,229	7,17,820
Area planted during 1st Five Year Plan (1951-56)				52,991
Area planted during 2nd Five Year Plan (1956-61)				17,926
Grand Total				7,41,040

Source: Department of Forest, Government of H.P.

Keeping in view the Forest Policy for Himachal Pradesh formulated in the year 1980 lays down that by 2000 A.D., the plantation programmes in the State was started right from the 1st Five Year Plan, but it was only from the 3rd Five Year Plan onwards that this programme received a real thrust. Total plantations of different species raised in the State 1961-62 onwards provide an idea regarding plantations being raised upto 1995-96. To make afforestation programme successful, plantation play a vital role. The figures with regard to new plantation of various varieties of trees in Himachal Pradesh Forests during 1992-93 to 1995-96 is reasonable impressive. There is a steady increase in covered area year after year. An overview of plantation schemes during this period gives a brief idea of the plantation of broad-leaved species in the Pradesh.

Further, a number of development programmes are proposed regarding plantation under Ninth Five Year Plan for forestry and soil conservation are carried out for raising of plantation and to arrest soil erosion in the catchments of important river basins. The proposed plantation schemes under Ninth Five Year Plan (1997-2002) under State and Central Sector are tabulated in Table 2.11.

TABLE 2.11: Proposed Plantation Schemes Under Ninth Five-Year Plan for Forestry and Soil Conservation Section (1997-2002)

Name of Schemes	Target	
	Physical area (in ha.)	Financial (Rs. in lacs)
1	2	3
A. Productive Forestry	(i) Forestry	
1. Quick growing species	19,600	2,500
2. Economic Plantation	21,700	2,700
3. Pasture Improvement	3,745	270
4. Social Forestry Programme	56,685	12,588
5. Fuel and Fodder Project	13,000	1,550
6. Other Afforestation	17,600	2,075
A. State Sector		
1. Protective Afforestation and Demonstration	6,000	2,000
B. Central Sector		
2. Soil Conservation in the catchments of river valley project (Beas and Satluj)	35,000	5,500
3. Integrated Watershed in the catchments FPR Giribata Pabbar	25,000	3,000

Source: Himachal Forest 1988, Forest Department, H.P.

Table 2.11 reveals the plantation schemes in view of productive forestry, quick growing species, economic plantation, pasture improvement, social forestry programmes, soil conservation and integrated watershed management. The figures provided for various plantation schemes are impressive both in physical and financial sector.

The scheme of quick growing species and economic plantation, an amount of rupees 2500 and 2700 (lacs) has been provided for the scheme with an objective to achieve physical area 19,600 and 21,700 (in hectares). Further, the social forestry programme and fuel fodder project have also been carried out effective figures. Under this scheme, the priority is given to afforestation scheme programmes.

Further, the soil conservation in the catchments of river-valley projects, comprehensive figures shows the priority in this area under the integrated watershed management in the catchments although Rs.3,000 lacs has been proposed but seems not upto mark.

Forest Working Plans—An Analysis

Out of total forest area 37,591 sq. kms. only 20,744 sq. kms have been brought under working plans. A working plan document is a tool of enforcing systematic, obligatory and mandatory regulations or continuous management of forest property. Working plans are prepared for every division to have continuity in the management and treatment to be given to the forests whose development particularly depends upon the quality of working plans and various prescriptions proposed, to be undertaken. Working plan is therefore, of great importance and have clearly enunciate the objective of management keeping in view the present policy of the government.

Forest working plans are usually prepared separately for each forest division, describing in detail the summary of basic facts on which the proposals are made and prescribing the methods for future management and detail prescription. There are 38 Forest Division in the State. These divisions are covered by 32 Working Plans. In addition, there are cantonment forests for which separate working plans prepared separately. A working plan is normally prepared for fifteen years period and it takes about 2 to 3 years to prepare this document. In this way at least two working plans prepared per year which means 5 to 6 plans should always be under preparation at a particular point of time.

Table 2.12 provides an idea of working plans and area as covered under working plans in H.P. by the Department of Forest.

To give proper orientation to the forest management to increase the tree growth and forest areas, the role of working plans in the State has an important approach to achieve the state policy objective. It is quite clear from the different working plans that a long term planning and effective strategies are the only way to achieve the desired goals to cover the maximum areas under plantations in the State. Working plans are prepared for every divisions is therefore, of great importance and should clearly enunciate the objective of management keeping in view the present policy of the Government.

Investment in Forest

Investment in Five Years Plans and Annual Plans is one of the important measures to assess the importance given to a particular segment of administration. It can also help in the assessment of the growth and development of a particular department and its activities. The Government of Himachal Pradesh and Department of Forest in particular has made significant achievements in the field of plan provisions for Forests in the State in the past few years. Table 2.13 gives the investment indices for forests during plans in Himachal Pradesh in the context of the total plan allocations.

Table 2.13 depicts that though in terms of figures investment on forests in Himachal Pradesh has registered a phenomenal increase from Rs.11.60 lakh during the plan period 1951-56 to the Plan period 1985-90 with investment of Rs.10445 lakh but in terms of per cent investment to the total plan outlay it has shown marginal increase only. There was stagnation, and even fall in investment during the plan periods available. It is only the Fourth Plan period and thereafter that has marginal increase. This again points to the possible divergence between the professed

TABLE 2.12: Working Plans and Areas Covered Under Different Working Plan

(Area in ha.)

Name of Forest Division	Name of Working Plan	Period of working plan	Area dealt within the working plan
1. Bilaspur	Revised W.P. for Bilaspur Forest Division	1975-76 to 1993-94	25,613
2. Hamirpur	W.P. for Hamirpur Forest Division	1981-82 to 1995-96	15,642
3. (i) Kunihar	Revised W.P. for Kunihar Forest Division	1977-78 to 1990-91	20,757
(ii) Nalagarh	Revised W.P. for Konica Forest Division	-do-	10,244
4. Chamba and Churah	Revised W.P. for Chamba Forest Division	1969-70 to 1983-84	67,401
5. Bharmaur Churah and Chamba	Revised W.P. for Dalhousie Forest Division	1969-70 to 1983-85	1,90,050
6. Pangi	W.P. for Pangi Forest Division	1964-65 to 1983-84	1,10,300
7. Dalhousie	Revised W.P. for Dalhausi Forest Division	1993-94 to 2007-2008	48,901
8. (i) Dharamshala	Revised W.P. for D/Shala Dehra (Part) Forest Division	1981-94 to 2007-2008	48,901
(ii) Dehra	(a) Revised W.P. for D/Shala Dehra (Part) Forest Division	-do-	20,475
	(b) Fifth W.P. of Forest of Una and Dehra (Part) Forest Division	1981-82 to 1995-95	9,590
9. Palampur	Revised W.P. for Palampur Forest Division	1981-82 to 1995-967	1,43,575
10. Nurpur	(a) W.P. for Nurpur Forest Division	1976-77 to 1990-91	40,678
	(b) Integrated W.P. of Co-operative Society Forest	1968-69 to 1983-84	7,819
11. Una	W.P. for Forest of Una and Dehra (Part) Forest Division	1981-82 to 1995-96	4,392
12. Kullu and Parbati	Revised W.P. for Kullu Forest Division	1979-80 to 1993-94	3,11,528
13. Seraja	W.P. for Seraj Forest Division	1986-87 to 2001-2002	1,04,820
14. Lahaul	Revised W.P. of Lahaul Forest Division	1993-94 to 2007-2008	6,13,691
15. Kotgarh Rampur	W.P. of Kotgarh Forest Division	1978-79 to 1992-93	56,272
16. Rampur	Fourth Revised W.P. for Kullu and Seraj Forest Division	1949-50 to 1979-80	25,066
17. Nichar and Pooh	W.P. of Kinnaur Forest Division	1976-77 to 1990-91	43,556
18. Shimla	(a) Revised W.P. for Shimla and Theog Forest Division	1981-82 to 1994-95	27,623
	(b) W.P. for Kunihar Forest Division (Part)	1977-78 to 1990-91	3,464
	(c) W.P. for Solan Forest Division	1977-78 to 1990-91	1,435
Theog	Revised W.P. for Shimla and Theog Forest Division	1981-82 to 1994-95	31,832

(*Contd.*)

Name of Forest Division	Name of Working Plan	Period of working plan	Area dealt within the working plan
19. Rohroo	Revised W.P. of Rohroo Forest Division	1969-90 to 1993-94	1,16,456
Jubbal	Revised W.P. of Rohroo Forest Division	-do-	29,531
20. Chopal	Revised W.P. for Chopal Forest Division	1980-81-1994-95	72,134
21. Nahan and Paonta	Revised W.P. of Rajgarh Forest Division	1982-83 to 1991-92	62,111
22. Rajgarh	Revised W.P. of Rajgarh Forest Division	1991-92 to 2005-2006	25,063
23. Renuka	Revised W.P. of Rajgarh Forest Division	1976-77 to 1990-91	25,063
24. Solan	W.P. for Solan Forest Division	1983-84 to 1997-98	14,374
25. Mandi Joginder Nagar	W.P. for Mandi Forest Division	1977-78 to 1991-92	41,167
26. Nachan	Revised W.P. of Mandi Forest Division	1977-78 to 1991-92	45,059
27. Suket	Revised W.P. for Suket Forest Division	1986-87 to 2000-01	34,582
28. Karsog	Revised W.P. for Karsog Forest Division	1986-87 to 1999-200	33,139
29. Kutlehar Jagir	W.P. for Kutlehar Forest Division	1961-62 to 1991-92	20,273
30. Subathu Cantonment	Revised W.P. for Cantonment	1991-92 to 2011-2012	105
31. Kasauli Cantonment	Revised W.P. for Kasauli Cantonment	1992-93 to 2011-2012	216
32. Dagshai Cantonment	Revised W.P. for Dagshai Cantonment	1993-94 to 2012-13	332
	Total Area covered under working plan		25,07,360

Source: H.P. Forest Statistics, 1996, Forest Department, Himachal Pradesh.

policy and the real practice of the State administration with regard to the afforestation stipulations. Table 2.14 also gives an idea of investment during the Annual Plans period 1992-93 to 1996-97 in Himachal Pradesh.

TABLE 2.13: Investment in Forest Under Five Year Plans

(Rs. in Lakhs)

Plan Period	Total Investment	Investment on Forest	Percentage of Forest Investment
1. First Plan 1951-56	527.25	11.60	2.20
2. Second Plan 1956-61	1,602.60	5.36	0.33
3. Third Plan 1961-62	3,384.47	40.39	1.19
4. Three Annual Plans 1966-67 to 1968-69	9,778.18	101.03	2.54
5. Fourth Plan 1969-74	11,342.97	793.92	6.70
6. Fifth Plan 1974-78	16,148.48	1,084.51	6.72
7. Annual Plan 1978-79 and 1979-80	14,755.53	802.00	5.44
8. Sixth Plan 1980-85	56,000.00	2830.00	5.05
9. Seventh Plan 1985-90	1,33,900.00	10445.00	7.80

Source: Government of Himachal Pradesh, Draft Seventh Plan (1985) Draft Annual Plan (1985-86), Planning Department, Shimla.

TABLE 2.14: Annual Plan Investment During 1992-93 to 1996-97 (Eighth Five-Year Plan)

Year	Total State Plan	Investment in Forestry and Soil Conservation Sector	Percentage allotment for forests on the total State Plan Outlay
1992-93	492.33	43.64	8.86
1993-94	570.72	37.71	6.61
1994-95	666.75	43.00	6.45
1995-96	835.00	51.58	6.18
1996-97	900.00	58.37	6.49

Source: Himachal Forests 1998, Forest Department, H.P.

It is quite clear from Table 2.14 that as far as investment in forestry and soil conservation in the State, there are sign of increase both in total State Plan and percentage in overall. Thus, the stipulations of State Forest Policy with regard to afforestation seem to be working in the desired direction. The another important area of environment conservation and development is related to soil conservation in the State keeping in view this broad objective, the department of forest, Government of Himachal Pradesh has taken certain provisions of investment in soil conservation in various Five Year Plans under State Sector and Central Sector. Table 2.15 gives an idea regarding the investment in different Five Year Plans and Annual Plans. The investment taken in State Sector and Central Sector is quite impressive in different plans. A general perusal of the figures shows a definite upturned in investment. Though the actual achievement will only be assessed at the

TABLE 2.15: Investment in Soil Conservation Under Five Year Plans (Central Sector)

(Rs. in Lakhs)

Plan Period	Under State Sector	RVP Scheme	Flood Prove	Other Schemes	Total Central Sector	Grand Total
First Plan (1951-56)	6.42	–	–	–	–	6.42
Second Plan (1956-61)	42.86	–	–	–	–	42.86
Third Plan (1966-67 to 1968-69)	189.09	264.21	–	–	264.21	453.30
Annual Plans (1966-67 to 1968-69)	51.25	151.12	–	–	151.12	202.37
Fourth Plan (1969-74)	135.56	261.86	–	–	261.86	397.42
Fifth Plan (1974-78)	163.97	275.87	–	8.00	283.89	447.86
Annual Plan (1978-79) and 1979-80	134.09	198.51	–	153.94	352.45	486.54
Sixth Plan (1980-85)	657.35	659.51	339.45	645.19	1,644.15	2,301.50
Annual Plan (1990-91)	112.38	260.17	195.19	6.00	461.36	573.74
Annual Plan (1991-92)	109.15	282.28	298.74	6.71	567.73	696.88
Eight Plan (1992-97)	875.00	4,000.00	2,400.00	–	6,400.00	7,275.00
Annul Plan (1992-93)	159.06	215.37	264.86	5.69	485.92	644.98
1993-94	147.12	301.16	277.68	6.87	505.71	732.83
1994-95	186.93	519.46	304.96	6.90	831.32	1,018.25
1995-96	201.57	431.39	228.29	10.60	670.28	871.85

Source: H.P. Forest Statistics, 1996, Forest Department, H.P.

conclusion of the plan, yet the intentions of the administration are quite evident from the statistics at least. It is quite clear from Table 2.15 that the State government has shown greater awareness to the need for quick and diversified afforestation and such other conservation schemes in view of the increasing danger of ecological imbalance.

Removal from Forests in Himachal Pradesh

In the past years, the yield has been prescribed on a conservative side. This has ranged between 7,50,000 cu/m (1975) to only 5,49,000 cu/m at present. Though, it could be of the older of 1 per cent of the growing stock, against average annual increment of 1.5 per cent i.e. about 10,00,000 cu/m.

It is evident that except during 1970, the total removals have been less than the prescribed yield. During 1975 and 1980, total removals were 4.70 lakh cu/m and 4.64 lakh cu/m as against prescribed yield of 7.50 lakh cu/m and 7.22 lakh cu/m respectively. During 1990 also the total removal were 4.35 lakh cu/m as against prescribed yield of 5.49 lakh cu/m. Thus, the whole approach has been conservation-oriented.

TABLE 2.16: Removal from Forest (1000 cu/m Standing Volume)

Name of Species	1970	1975	1980	1985	1990	1995
Deodar	1,50,129	1,07,381	77,724	1,28,337	63,220	
Kail	1,44,684	80,904	1,29,204	71,394	63,685	
Chil	1,36,526	87,394	83,018	1,24,393	13,903	
Fir/Spruce	1,91,749	1,21,823	1,51,913	1,07,758	1,52,256	
Sal	34,415	-	8,781	16,321	3,183	
Other Broad Leaved	23,093	73,057	13,065	12,006	14,239	
Total	6,80,596	4,70,559	4,63,705	4,60,209	4,35,586	4,50,000

Source: State of the Environment Report, H.P. March 2000.

According to the State percentage of Forest report 1995(FSI) the total growing stock is an area of 12501 sq. kms which has a density of 10 per cent and above, is 25.44 crore cu/m and the annual increment is 16.77 lac cu/m. In view of this position and the fact that felling are necessary, the Himachal Pradesh Government has reviewed its decision to ban commercial green felling and approved the silvicultural fellings as per the working plans prescriptions. This is as under:

(1) ***Regeneration felling:*** This felling is required to be carried out in periodic block I areas in the form of seeding and final felling. The purpose of these felling is to open the canopy and make a seed bed for natural and artificial regeneration.
(2) ***Thinning Felling:*** Thinning fellings are required to be carried out in Periodic Block IV, Periodic Block III and Periodic Block II areas to remove congestion.
(3) ***Selection Marking:*** These are required to be carried out in areas allotted to Selection Working Circles, where mature trees over a certain diameter are required to be removed.

However, the above approval is subject to the Hon'ble Supreme Court orders who are seized of the matter in a public interest litigation and would like to green fellings to be done on the basis of Working Plans approved by the Government of India and norms fixed by an Expert Committee specially constituted for the purpose.

Depletion of Forest Cover: An Analysis

The various figures available regarding the various classes of forests in Himachal Pradesh shows that the land covered by forests has decreased in certain forest sector. The area under reserved forests and protected forests has remained undisturbed due to government policy to protect thick forest areas. But there are other various forest sectors, which has been tremendously decreased due to various reasons in Himachal Pradesh. Although realizing the importance of forests, especially hilly area like Himachal Pradesh steps are taken in recent years for controlling the denudation and revising forests through certain forestry programmes in the State. The Department of Forest although working hard to maintain and achieve the forest policy in the State has implemented various plantation schemes on vacant places through the co-operation of the local people at local level.

Since the commencement of various projects, the Himachal Pradesh Forest Department has brought a large area under this scheme. But it is also significant to know that due to number of factors a fairly sharp decline in some forest sector has been examined from data available. Table 2.17 analysis the resultant changes in various classes of forests from 1971-72 to 1994-95 in Himachal Pradesh.

Table 2.17 explains the various factors relating to depletion of forests in various sectors in Himachal Pradesh as mentioned earlier. The table analysis the forest area in view of reserved, protected, and unclassed, private and other forests. It is quite clear from the data available that only reserved and protected forests from the year 1971-72 to 1995-96 have been equally maintained and protected by the Department of Forest. The figures highlights that during the various years there is nothing much disturbance or interference to such forests, reasons that there is no any type of relaxation to disturb these protected forests from human and animal activities. Although, there is a slight increase in protected forests areas upto 1995-96, that is 31,453 sq. kms where it was only 17,329 sq. kms during the year 1971-72. This only possible through the advancement of new plantation made by different working plans available to different forest divisions keeping in view the importance of broad leaved trees in the State.

Further, it is also observed that it is only the unclassed forest area where the figures show depletion in forest after year 1991-92 onwards. In Himachal Pradesh, this is the area where all the pressures have been developed by a number of factors. The massive illicit felling is one of the main reasons to this sector. There are other activities which normally becoming the causes of depletion to unclassed forests such as urbanization, industrialization, constructions, encroachment and commercialization of forests by the State Government.

It is also observed that the private forests are also decreased due to certain reasons. The area, which was 562 sq. kms. during the year 1971-72, is reduced to 404 sq. kms. in 1995-96. The figures available provide an idea regarding the marginal increase in forests in other sector of forest. This is only possible to the State Government due to the people's participation through different schemes.

TABLE 2.17: Resultant Changes in Various Classes of Forest 1971-72 to 1994-95 (Area in sq. kms.)

Particulars	1971-72	1976-77	1981-82	1984-85	1985-86	1986-87	1987-88	1988-89	1990-91	1991-92	1992-93	1994-95	1995-96
1. Reserve Forest	1864	1826	1825	1825	1896	1896	1896	1896	1896	1896	1896	1896	1896
2. Protected Forest	1732	17704	17129	17196	33454	33471	33448	33449	33449	33449	33165	31472	31453
3. Unclassed Forest	762	742	731	910	909	893	872	868	868	868	634	680	680
4. Private Forest	562	666	553	493	493	533	533	569	529	529	450	404	404
5. Others	920	904	904	901	947	908	908	908	947	947	915	953	993
Total	21487	21482	21142	37701	21325	37701	37691	37792	37591	37591	37062	35407	35427

Source: State of the Environment Report—Himachal Pradesh, March 2000.

Forest Fires: Degradation of Biodiversity and Productivity

Forest fires play a major role in degradation of biodiversity and productivity of forests. It is estimated that about 60 per cent of forest area is damaged by repeated annual forest fires. Forest fires are quite common and widespread since time immemorial. Today, the incidence of forest fires is very high due to increase in biotic interference in the forest eco-system and inadequate forest fire management practices. Decreasing fiscal allocation in forestry sector and change in our priorities towards the whole concept of systematic forest fire management are among the more important factors for failure in prevention of forest fires.

More than 92 per cent of forests in India are government owned and the responsibility of forest management, including that of preventing forest fires, lies with the State Forest Department. Therefore, a national plan for systematic forest fire management for the purposes of guiding, co-ordinating and monitoring the activities in this regard is necessary to realize national goals and objectives. The National Forest Policy, 1988, also clearly spelt out the need for protecting forest fires through "Special precautions to be taken during the fire seasons and improved and modern management practices adopted to deal with forest fire." Amongst various factors, which cause forest fires, the following are:

(i) Fires are caused deliberately by labourers collecting non-timber forest produce
(ii) Fires left smouldering by the negligence of labourers/ pedestrians/ graziers, etc.
(iii) By way of vengeance of villagers
(iv) Deliberately setting forest on fire by villagers with a view to getting fresh blade of grass for their animal as fodder.

Fire in forest has been a perpetual problem though never tackles seriously. Even today, there is no co-ordination between forest department and other agencies like National Remote Sensing Agency (NRSA), India Meteorological Department (IMD) and Forest Survey of India (FSI). The Department does not have the requisite resources to fight the fires. Table 2.18 shows the causes of forest fires incidences in Himachal Pradesh from 1991-92 to 1997-98.

Table 2.18 provides the figures relating to the causes of forest fire along with number of cases and affected areas. Though forest fire is a global phenomenon, the only difference in tackling this problem in Himachal Pradesh is the lack of prioritization of forest management objectives. The concept of forestry planning has changed over the period of time with the changing fund planning. Earlier, most of the forest activities were funded through non-plan, therefore, the funding source was stable and assured, but soon after the introduction of plan funding in the forestry sector, the maintenance components of forests, which included many issues (fire protection being one of them) were given up.

The figures related to forest fires from 1991-92 to 1997-98 in Himachal Pradesh shows that the number of cases and area has been reduced from last few years. This reduction has been possible only through the environmental education and people participation and awareness in the rural masses. The another area of prevention and control of the forest fire in the state depends on two basic components:

(i) Control burning,
(ii) Clearing of forest lines.

In hilly forest areas the effective way to check forest fire expansion are maintenance of fires lines, block lines, installation of adequate watch tower, networking through wireless communication system and a highly mobile fire-fighting crew to reach the nearest sight of fire by road. Table 2.19 provides an idea of area protected by the Forest Department from the fire:

If the forest fire protection schemes in Himachal Pradesh is analysed, it may be found that the project progressed in an effective way. The area protected from fire has increased 30,36,971 ha. in 1997-98 whereas it was only just 9,57,668 ha. in the year 1983-84. Therefore, if proper planning and adequate homework would have been done the result can be obtained in progressed line.

International consultants team of FAO gave a detailed technical report underlining the grim situation of forest fire in India. The report points out:

TABLE 2.18: Causes of Forest Fires

Cases	1991-92		1992-93		1993-94		1994-95		1995-96		1996-97		1997-98	
	Cases	Area	Cases	Area	Cases	Area	Cases	Area	Cases	Area	Cases	Area	Cases	Area
1	2	3	4	5	6	7	8	9	10	11	12	13	14	15
Fire caused by accident	93	2157	96	1732	46	569	16	127	58	4165	28	421	14	1993
Fire entering the forests by crossing exterior fire traces	12	744	16	205	5	144	5	160	15	599	6	30	2	8
By villagers/travellers etc. passing through the forests	331	2257	127	2597	348	7188	1603	9509	1315	41748	120	1250	29	143
Institutional firing causes unknown	96	1167	86	3245	187	2269	82	9	1054	281	6562	–	–	0
Total	532	6325	325	7779	586	10170	10850	1669	53174	154	1701	50	50	2144

Source: Annual Reports of Forest Department, Himachal Pradesh.

TABLE 2.19: Area Protected from Forest Fire in Himachal Pradesh

Years	Area attempted to be protected	Failures i.e. area actually to be pointed	Area protected	Protection cost (Rs. million)
0	1	2	3	4
1983-84	9,58,628	966	9,57,668	0,379
1984-85	9,74,671	50,364	9,24,307	3,563
1993-94	18,71,178	10,170	18,61,008	2,650
1994-95	26,80,912	10,850	26,70,062	3,033
1996-97	26,89,223	6,052	26,83,171	9,399
1997-98	30,39,145	2,174	30,36,971	8,942

Source: Annual Administrative Reports, Forest Department, H.P.

> "Fire situation in India is alarming. There is no focus on forest fire in India. In economic or ecological term, and curriculums of forester's training at all level are rather inadequate in fire science and technology. There is no clear fire strategy or an awareness of strategic planning. Fire management is only now beginning to engage the attention of planners and the awareness of fire effects on the forest economy is severely limited. Statistical data on forest fires, where available, are either skeletal or unreliable, as these data are not the output of a system of recording. No system exists for fire weather forecasting, danger rating, fire reporting or preventive measures apart from some basic fire line clearance and prescribed burning on plantation boundaries. India's forests deserve a full-fledged fire management system institutionalized at the state level with strategic inputs of training, research, and awareness building coming from the Central Government."

Another Committee, headed by R.D. Khosla, which was constituted by Ministry of Environment and Forests after a massive fire in the Himachal Pradesh in 1995 suggested an answer of remedial measures for five protections. Some of these were:

(i) Increase vigilance is necessary by appointment of an adequate number of firewatchers during the month of April, May and June as used to be the practice earlier.

(ii) Clearing and maintenance of fire lines virtually abandoned of late due to shortage of funds must be carried out regularly.

(iii) The practice of control burning to deal with the accumulation of combustible pine needles on the forest floor is reintroduced.

(iv) Efforts for finding alternative uses for pine needles should be supported by the government so as to demonstrate their economic viability. This will help reduce the accumulation of combustible material on the forest floor.

(v) The forest department staff should be provided with a complete communication network through wireless to enable a quick response in dealing with forest fire and also illicit felling of trees.

(vi) The communication network should be supported with improved mobility to enable quick transport of men and material from one area to another. For this at least one additional jeep may be provided at the divisional level to the D.F.O. in the hill area.

(vii) To whether villagers come to assist the Forest Department in extinguishing forest fires or not, their timber rights should not be curtailed or forfeited.

(viii) The state government must ensure that adequate funds are provided to the Forest Department for the proper care, maintenance and protection of the forest. These funds should be provided through a centrally sponsored scheme for this purpose.

Keeping in view the above-recommended factors for fire protection in Himachal Pradesh, the department of forest has taken various tools and techniques to check the fire and the result has been achieved in the State.

Watershed Management: An Integrated Approach

Watershed is defined as a natural hydrological entity that covers a specific area expanse of land surface within whose boundaries the entire rainfall-runoff ultimately passes through a specifically defined stream. Watershed characterization requires generation and gathering of precise information on a number of parameters of both static and dynamic in nature comprising of geology, geomorphology, hydrology, soils, land use/land cover, soil erosion, climate etc. The management of watershed may take place in the form of land-use planning, construction of conservation work, water harvesting, afforestation etc. In India Integrated Watershed Development Programme has been conceived for holistic development of farming system and land-use planning in recent years.

Integrated Watershed Development Project (Hills) Himachal Pradesh, was launched in January 1991 with a financial outlay of Rs.9.49 million (36.76 crore at the credit availability).[49] Later on the total outlay was increase to Rs.49.19 crore. The forest department is the nodal agency for Himachal Pradesh, which is executing the project with assistance of other line departments like agriculture, horticulture and animal husbandry. The project extends over five rivers watersheds of Markanda, Ghaggar, Sirsa, Swan and Chakki with a total area of 3,013 sq. kms. Out of the total area falling in the catchments of this watershed, around 75,000 ha. comprising of 27 sub-watersheds have been taken up during the project period.

The main objective of the project is to slow and reverse degradation of the natural environment through the use of appropriate soil and moisture conservation technology. In the process of conserving soil and moisture, it improves the production and income from the grain crops, horticulture, fodder, fiber, fuelwood and livestock and reduces flooding in adjacent plains.

This aim is to lay the foundation for sustainable increase in production to keep pace with the population growth. The project promotes known vegetative technologies and verifies others, develops approaches for co-ordinated inter-active planning and strengthens the management and use of non-arable lands.

The overall aims of the project are:

(i) to slow and reverse the degradation of natural environment through the use of appropriate soil and moisture conservation technology,

(ii) to conserve soil and water,

(iii) to increase and improve the production and income from crops, horticulture, fodder, fiber, fuelwood and livestock through the process of soil and water conservation

(iv) to reduce flooding and devastation caused by degradation of soil.

Project Implementation

A steering committee has been established at the State level to review and sanction new sub-watershed plans, annual programmes and to approve supporting budget. It also reviews the progress reports and resolves the problems of project implementation. The Commissioner-cum-Secretary Forest is the Chairperson of this Committee. Secretaries and heads of line departments like forest, agriculture, horticulture, animal husbandry and Director of Research, State Agriculture Universities as well as Advisor Planning Secretary Finance are the other members of the Committee. The Project Director is the member-secretary of the committee.

The Headquarters are located at Solan with field units at Nahan, Nalagarh, Una and Nurpur.

Table 2.20 analyse the component-wise expenditure made by the project in the State on various sectors.

TABLE 2.20: Component-wise Expenditure

A. Field Operations (72%) of Total	
(i) Horticulture	5 to 10% of Field Operation
(ii) Agriculture	10 to 15% of field operation
(iii) Forestry	30 to 35% of Field Operation
(iv) Animal husbandry	10 to 12 % of Field Operation
(v) Drainage and Water Management	35 to 40 % of Field Operation
B. Operation Cost	28% of total

Source: Forest Survey of India.

The expenditure explained in Table 2.20 shows that the project is also providing a healthy investment on forestry sector ranges between 30 to 35 per cent. This gives the picture of priority to the environment conservation and development in the State.

People's Participation

About 1.4 lakh people forming 22,886 families live in the 27 sub-watersheds covered under the project. Most of these areas are rain fed and before the intervention of the project the socio-economic condition of these people was very poor. Irrigation facilities were lacking and only about 10 per cent of the total arable area was under irrigation.

The IWDP implements its activities with participation of the local people who are the main direct beneficiaries of the project. The people have constituted themselves into 104 Village Development Committees with an elected executive body of 10 to 12 members. They maintain a bank account and detailed minutes are kept for the meetings of each executive committee and general body.

Levels of Participation

The levels of participation of VDC as well as individual members are indicated below:

(i) In horticulture the stakeholders have changed from 30 per cent to 80 per cent. This is mainly in the form of labour.

(ii) In afforestation on private lands, the stakeholders share has been increased from 10 to 15 per cent mainly in the form of labour.

(iii) In agriculture component the stakeholder's share has risen from 20 to 30 per cent mainly as labour.

(iv) There is no fixed norm for levels of participation in water harvesting structures and drainage line treatment.

(v) Animal husbandry dispensaries are constructed on land given by the local population.

Role of Panchayats

At present there is no formal institutional arrangement for the role of panchayats in the VDCs. However, in many cases the role is complementary and supplementary. Panchayats see the VDCs as their local watershed management unit and members of Panchayats are often office-bearers of the VDCs.

Gone are the days when forests in Himachal Pradesh used to be the major source of revenue. In the present day scenario pressure on forests has increased due to increase in population and the main objectives of forest management has shifted from revenue generation to meet the genuine need of the local people. The forest policy of Government of India, 1988, has clearly stated that forest needs of the local people should be given priority over revenue generation. With the change in the policy mandate there has been a thrust on involvement of local people in forest management, to give them sense of belongingness.

Although local people in Himachal Pradesh have already been informally involved in forest protection for last many years. The concept behind the people's participation is definitely to meet the forest-based needs of the village communities along with sustainable development of forest resources. Various components of the scheme laid emphasis on involvement of village communities in development and protection of forest resources. Social forestry like many other developmental programmes was launched with the basic initiative coming from the government under certain prevailing ecological and socio-economic conditions, as perceived by planners and policy-makers. Government laid down certain objectives and guidelines for the programme fully provided the lands required for its implementation resting with the State controlled Forests department, which invited the people to participate in it. In this sense, the peoples' participation was mere a programme participation, the initiative and execution being primarily governmental with very little dependence on people's capacity and resources.

During the project period, local people were involved in various forestry programmes, under various components of Social Forestry Umbrella Project. Response of local community was quite encouraging, and various Village Development Committee (VDCs) formed under the project worked very well towards protection and development of forests. With the termination of project in 1993, these committee so formed also stopped working. The main reason for these committees becoming defunct in the absence of project aid appears to be the target-oriented approach. Main thrust was given on achievement of targets. Sustenance of the programmes, which started during the project period, was not given attention. Forest Department staff was used to doing the protection of forest through policing attitude, whereas, people's participation required change in attitude of the staff and capacity building of staff practicing new approaches. Thrust was on implementation of the scheme, so the tracing aspect was not given importance to the level required for the changed working. So, during project period the scheme produced very good results, but these could not sustain after the project.

'Van Lagao, Rozi Kamao' was another scheme to ensure participation of local people in Forestry programmes. The scheme which started in 1992, aimed at increasing green cover in the State after utilizing the available resources. Main thrust in the scheme was to evolve local people in protection of plantations for getting optimum results. Another objective of the scheme was to provide employment to the poor people. Plantations under Social Forestry Umbrella Project from 1991-92 were brought under this Yojana. Poorest of the poor beneficiaries were selected and employed as 'Van Sewaks'. Their involvement in forest protection was ensured by the payments with survival per cent of the plantation ensured their involvement in forest protection. This scheme could not go along way due to certain unavoidable circumstances at Government level and sudden stoppage of funds.

Joint Forest Management: Idea and Action

For hill state like Himachal Pradesh the decline in forest cover has been alarming. It is now increasingly realized that the Forest Department alone is not capable of protecting the forests of the State. It is also understood that the local communities at present are also not sufficiently sensitized to manage the forest without any support. With success stories emerging from all parts of the country it appears that Joint Forest Management (JFM) is the best strategy to rehabilitate the degraded forests patches and protect them.

In 1993, Government of Himachal Pradesh issued a notification regarding implementation of Joint Forest Management in the State. Formal process of initiation of practicing JFM started in Kullu and Mandi Forest Circles with the implementation of project on JFM, funded by ODA (Oversees Development Administration), of U.K. in September 1994. ODA project was different from other projects, in which there was flexibility of incorporating changes on the basis of experience gained during working with the approach. Pilot phase of this project, which was for a period of three years, aimed at testing the JFM approach in selected pilot locations for its further replication in whole of Kullu and Mandi circle and then in whole of Himachal Pradesh.

Initiation of JFM process requires change in attitude of forest staff from traditional policing one to a friendly facilitator. So, project lays a lot of emphasis on capacity building of staff and attitudinal change to practice this approach. In order to achieve this, project was categorized into three main components:

(i) ***Institutional Development:*** By providing project support to activities like modern equipments to increase efficiency in working, vehicles to increase mobility and through trainings by upgrading the training institutes of DFFC and training in UK and in India.

(ii) ***Joint Forest Planning and Management:*** As per government of Himachal Pradesh Guideline of May 12, 1993 including various capacity building programmes for staff and local people.

(iii) ***Forestry Operation:*** Which lays emphasis on basic forestry activities like natural regeneration, artificial regeneration, regeneration surveys, subsidiary silvicultural operations, fire protection measures, seed stand for obtaining quality seed, and demonstration plots for demonstrating various forestry practices.

The Village Forest Development Committee (VFDC) was provided the responsibility of rehabilitation and management of degraded forest area, assigned under the control of concerned Panchayat. The parameters of performance of each committee must be decided and adopted after mutual discussion with the line department, i.e., forest department in the case of VFDC. These parameters include:

(a) The survival percentage of plantations raised under JFM.
(b) Prevention of forest fires in the defined jurisdiction of VFDC.
(c) Checking of illicit removal of forests produce and the help rendered to the forest department in this regard.
(d) Sharing of benefits among all the beneficiaries without giving rise to conflicts or managing the conflicts locally.
(e) Control of misuse of TD timber.
(f) Control of illegal hunting of wildlife and help rendered to the forest department, etc.

The forests of Himachal Pradesh, and the people and sectors that depend upon them, are subject to increasing change. However, the policy and institutional framework for forestry is not suited to many new conditions and needs. As a result, the right mix of forest goods and services distributed fairly recognizing this, the H.P. Forest Department (HPFD) called for a comprehensive Forest Sector Review (FSR).[50] Recognising also that the information base is poor, the FSR was based firmly on multi-stakeholder consultations and expert focus groups organized by the HPFD, facilitated by IIED (An international, independent policy research group) and funded by DFID-India (British Development Assistance), the FSR provides the first comprehensive big picture of Himachal Pradesh forest sector.

It presents finding on the physical status, use, economics, laws, institutions and policies concerning the valuable forest asset base. Moreover, it offers recommendations for policy and institutional change—recommendations that have the weight of widespread participation behind them. These recommendations emphasize continuing participation, strengthening of local institutions so that they become effective forest stewards, finding ways to realize the high forest values to help social and economic development, and thoroughly updating the HPFD as a facilitating expert service.

Since the FSR serve as a 'bridge' between understanding the present and defining a future vision, it is necessary to devise an analytical framework which assess the current situation in relation to possible future needs for sustainable forest management through several key areas and specialist work and institutions set up includes:

- Village Forest Development Committees (VDCs) developed under DFO H.P. Forestry Project;
- Village Development Committee (VDCs) under the Indo-German Changer Project (IGCP) and the Integrated Watershed Development Project (IWDP),
- Village Eco-Development Committee (VDCs) under the Great Himalayan National Park,
- Village Forest Development Societies (VFDSs) or Sanghi Van Samiti (SVS) formed under Sanjhi Van Yojana.

All these village level institutions came into existence on an ad hoc basis with the projects and were formed according to the different mandates and activities within each projects.

Initially, the Forest Guard was made the Member-Secretary of these village level institutions. This was to ensure effective management of funds, record keeping and equip community members to take over responsibilities. The village forest institutions relating to local level forest conservation and development involved are:

Forest Co-operatives: There were first formed in 1941, and received grant-in-aid until 1971.

Informal Jungle or Protection Committee: These have, on occasion, emerged to respond to a specific crisis or sudden change in forest management, which affects their livelihood e.g., extreme degradation of nearby forests, lack or absence of response from HPFD in resolving conflicts or responding to community needs.

Gram Panchayat (GP): GP has played a rather indecisive role in forest development and management. Although, an organized and legally acceptable body, its functions and priorities are essentially for local self-governance. GPs actively participate in certifying TD applications of individual households.

Non-Forest Local Institutions: In addition to the forest specific village institution and Gram Panchayats, there are many other types of institutions such as Mahila Mandals, Youth Groups, Devta Committees, Village Education Committees, Self-Help Groups, Farmers Clubs, Parent-Teacher Associations, Mother Teacher Associations, Village Committees, and Panchayats Raj Institutions (PRIs). Many of these play forest role.

Village Forest Institutions—A Critical Review

Although most village forest institutions are of comparatively recent origins, they have brought greater focus on forest issues—plantation on degraded forest land, fire protection, soil conservation and silvi-pasture activities have been given boost, illicit felling and smuggling had decreased—and that overall awareness of the need for protection and conservation of forests had increased. In addition, it is also analysed that the work gets done faster through village forest institutions, avoiding the long procedural delays associated with the panchayat system. The formation of these institutions has involved process of coalescence of people around tangible issues and, most importantly, participation in the work being done. This in spite of considerable recent progress in involving community organisations in forest management, there is still much to be sorted out regarding local level governance to achieve equitable and sustainable benefits from forests.

3

Environment Pollution Management

The Himachal Pradesh State Environment Protection and Pollution Control Board was constituted in the year 1975 under the provision of Water (Prevention and Control of Pollution) Act, 1974. Subsequently, the implementation of Water (Prevention and Control of Pollution) Cess Act, 1977; Air (Prevention and Control of Pollution) Act, 1981; The Environment (Protection) Act, 1986 and Public Liability Insurance Act, 1991 was also entrusted to preserving the wholesomeness of quality of environment and prevention of hazards to human beings, terrestrial and aquatic flora and fauna. The State Board is involving in the following broad sectors:

- Placing comprehensive programmes for the prevention, control or abatement of pollution in the State.
- Advising State government relating to environmental aspects.
- Collecting and disseminating information relating to environment.
- To enforce various provisions of the environment protection Acts to keep the quality of environment in a healthy condition.
- The State Board is also encouraging Self-Regulating Order by industries association to control the pollution.

The United Nations Stockholm Conference on the Human Environment held on June 5, 1972 was a landmark in the direction of environmental preservation in which the UN Member States including India resolved for the preservation of the natural resources on the earth. The resolution adopted in the conference included amongst other things, the preservation of the quality and wholesomeness of air and water which are vital to support and sustain the life of this planet.

Environmental protection today is a major problem of the present society. Man's desire for ultimate joy and comfort has led him to exploit nature's free goods to the extent of reducing its natural capacities for self-stabilization. In almost all societies, man has been continuously and indiscriminately manipulating the environment and nature to gain its end. In the process man has almost left the environment badly mould and mutilated, which has proved harmful to the humanity itself. As a consequence of the outright disregard of the impact of these activities, numerous environmental problems have arisen.

A protection of environment is thus a major global problem and cannot be tackled in violation by each country. Pollution of air, space, land areas and oceans is taking place rapidly. Because of the application of global technology, there are ecological changes occurring in the structure of the earth with a adverse impact on global environment.

In order to keep the commitment the union of India promulgated various Acts and Rules with the prime objective of regulating the economic growth within the precincts of sustainable development. The following statutes are important as far as the role and functions of the State Environment Protection and Pollution Control Board are concerned:

(1) *Water (Prevention and Control of Pollution) Act, 1974*

The Parliament in the 25th year of the Republic promulgated this legislation in pursuance to clause 1 of Article 242 of the Constitution of India, with the objective of prevention and control of water pollution and maintenance and restoration of wholesomeness of waster. The H.P. State Environment Protection and Pollution Control Board was constituted in 1974 under the provision of the Act.

(2) *Water (Prevention and Control of Pollution) Cess Act, 1977*

This Act provide for levy of cess on the water consumed for specified purposes with a view to dissuade wasteful and indiscreet use of water. The cess proceeds so raised are intended to be utilized for programmes related to control of water pollution besides augmenting the resources of the State Pollution Control Boards.

(3) *Air (Prevention and Control of Pollution) Act, 1981*

On the analogy of Water (Prevention and Control of Pollution) Act, 1974 the Union Government promulgated another identical legislation which was exclusively meant to deal with the problems of air quality and preservation and maintenance thereof.

(4) *Environment (Protection) Act, 1986*

In order to provide the existing legislation for control of water and air pollution more effectively and to remove the deficiency of these legislation, the Union Government enacted another umbrella legislation in 37th year of Republic. The prime objective of the legislation was to plug the existing statutory gaps.

(5) *Manufacture, Storage and Import of Hazardous Chemical Rules, 1989*

These rules specify the regulatory procedures for safe production, handling and use of hazardous chemicals.

(6) *Hazardous Waste (Management and Handling) Rules, 1989*

These rules spell out the procedures and restrictions on handling, treatment and disposal of hazardous wastes in various industrial processes and other developmental activities.

(i) Rules for Manufacture, Use, Import and Storage of Hazardous Micro-Organisms, Genetically Engineered Micro-Organism or Cells, 1989: These rules provide for regulation on safe use, import and storage of hazardous micro-organism, genetically engineered micro-organism or cells for various industrial and developmental purposes.

(ii) Procedure for Environmental Clearance: In all 29 categories of developmental projects have been notified by Government of India in the Notification No. SO (60)E dated 27.01.94/04.05.94 and Notification No. SO 318(E) dated 10.04.97 issued under Environment Protection Act, 1986 in which the State Pollution Control Board has a key role to perform as a facilitator and regulator.

Public Liability Insurance Act, 1991

This Act mainly provides for covering and compensating the public risks due to hazardous industrial and developmental activities. All the specified projects required to obtain an insurance cover under this Act.

The main functions and activities of the State Pollution Control Board are performed within the ambit of the aforesaid Acts, Rules and Regulations. The scope and mandate of these statutes is ever increasing in view of the emerging public concerns about the environment.[51]

Functions of the State Board

The fact is that it is the State Board which look after the improvement in the air quality and to prevent and control air pollution. The State Board has been assigned the following functions towards environmental conservation and development in the State:

(a) to plan a comprehensive programme for retention, control or abatement of air and power pollution and to secure to execution thereof;

(b) to advise State Government on any matter concerning the prevention, control or abatement of air pollution;

(c) to collect and disseminate information relating to water pollution and prevention, control or abatement thereof;

(d) to collect and disseminate information relating to air and water pollution;

(e) to encourage, conduct and participate in investigations and research relating to water and air pollution and prevention, control or abatement of water and air pollution;
(f) to inspect air and water pollution control areas at such intervals as it may think necessary, assess the quality of air therein and take steps for prevention, control or abatement of air pollution in such areas;
(g) to inspect, sewage or trade/industrial effluents, works and plans for the treatment of sewage and effluents;
(h) to review plans, specifications or other data relating to plants set up for the treatment of water works for the purification thereof and the system for the disposal of sewage or trade industrial effluents or in connection with the grant of any consent as required by the Water Act;
(i) to lay down, in consultation with Central Board and heavy regard to the standards for the quality of air laid down by the Central Board, Standards for emission of air pollutants into the atmosphere from industrial plants and automobiles or for the discharge of any air pollutant into the atmosphere from any other source whatever, not being a ship or an aircraft;
(j) to advise the State Government with respect to suitability of any premises or locations for carrying on any industry which is likely to cause air pollution;
(k) to evolve economical and reliable methods of sewage and industrial effluents;
(l) to make, vary or revoke any order for the prevention, control of abatement of discharges of waste into streams or wells; and
(m) to lay down effluent standards to be complied with by persons while causing discharge of sewage or sullage or both and to lay down, modify or annul effluent standards for the sewage and trade effluents.

Organizational Structure

The State Board was constituted in the year 1975, with its headquarters at Shimla along with 10 regional offices, a central laboratory and three Regional Laboratories, which are catering to the diverse requirements in terms of environmental monitoring, surveillance and analysis of complex environmental parameters.

The Board is headed by the Chairperson and Commissioner-cum-Secretary (ST & E) with the help of Member-Secretary for overall management and control of the organisation. The Board is assisted by an Environment Engineer (HQ), Senior Scientific Officer, Environment Geologist and Senior Project Consultant for efficient and effective functioning of the Board. The Board has a Law Officer for legal consultation. Further, the Board is also assisted by Assistant Controller (E&A), Assistant Environment Engineer (HQ) and Project Consultant.

The H.P. State Pollution Control Board has a small organizational structure with a total strength of 82 persons in all. However, during the last few years the Board has made dramatic upsurge in its activities and has made credible achievements in terms of organizational revamping as well as in physical achievements.

The Board has adopted a major shift in its policy from purely regulatory set up to an interactive scientific organisation undertaking the role of technology transfer seeking persuasive involvement of industry through consultative mechanism. Some of the innovative programmes of the Board are as follows:[52]

(i) Perpetuated financial sufficiency in the fourth successive year.

(ii) Consultancy wing continue to carry out diagnostic studies and provide know-how on environmental technologies.

(iii) Installation of treatment facilities in 100 per cent of the polluting industries in the State. Efforts to regulatory monitor their efficacious operation and upgradation is now on.

(iv) Continued Operation Cleantech a project to provide know-how for process modifications to eliminate discharge of pollutants at source rather than the conventional end of the pipe treatment.

(v) Promoted the concept of installation of technology demonstration project, which would ensure a zero discharge industry under cleantech.

(vi) Launched a formal waste exchange to facilitate reprocessing of industrial waste for value addition to prevent pollution. Waste minimization circles are being established at local levels with the involvement of industry and NGOs.

(vii) To introduce innovative concept of public learning to resolve serious complaints and decide locations of polluting industries.

(viii) First State Board in the country to revise and implement the emission standards for boilers and mini and major cement plants.

(ix) The Board signed MOU with Ministry of Non-Conventional Energy Sources for setting up Bioreactors for Vegetable/municipal solid Waste at Shimla. Negotiation for setting up similar plant at Mandi and treatment facility for abattoir at Shimla is in progress.

(x) Technical Activities Accomplished:

  (a) Preparation of Zoning Atlas for locating polluting industries, Solan Atlas completed and Una, Sirmour under preparation.

  (b) Preparation of district level disaster management plans. Completed for Solan district and district Una plan under preparation.

  (c) Feasibility study for dumping site for hazardous wastes at Baddi completed. Study for district Sirmour under preparation. Proposal for funding the project already submitted to Government of India.

  (d) Inventorisation of hazardous waste already completed for the entire state for setting up dumping sites and preparation of disaster management plans.

  (e) Launch a survey to assess environmental impact of mining activities on aquifers. A regular mining division to evaluate environment management plans for mining projects is proposed to be set up.

(f) Organized more than 50 vehicular monitoring camps in the State to ensure the environmental Standards for the vehicular emissions are kept within limits.

(g) Under Mass Awareness Programme organized publicity campaign about environmental technology and its application and Cleaner Manufacturing Technologies, 150-14000 Environment Management System, Waste Minimization through Adoption of Cleaner Technologies in Hotels and Restaurants and Food Processing Industries. The Board also organized techno show to demonstrate modern control monitoring and analytical technologies.

(h) Inventorisation of polluting small scale industries in the State of H.P.

(i) Inventorisation of large and medium (Water and Air) polluting industries in the State of H.P.

(j) Survey of Urban Municipal Waste in Shimla, Mandi and Dharamshala.

(k) Adoption of clear technologies for small-scale industries and demonstration projects for strictly isolated units.

(l) Industrial estate survey for the State of H.P. is completed and updating is being done as an ongoing activity.

Air Pollution: Boards' Effort in Controlling Air Pollution

According to Environment Protection Act (1986), environment includes water, air, land and their inter-relationship with human beings, other living creatures, plants and microorganisms. Air pollution is the state of environment in which the inter-ambient atmosphere contains gases and other materials in concentrations which are harmful to man and environment.

The Air (Prevention and Control of Pollution) Act, 1981, defines "Air Pollutant" and the reference to them defines air pollution.

"Air Pollutant" means any solid, liquid or gaseous substance present in the atmosphere in such concentration as may be or lead to injurious to human beings or other living creatures.

In India especially the big cities are having the problem of air pollution on account of concentration of industries and power plants. In pursuant to the Stockholm Conference, India passed the Air (Control and Prevention of Pollution) Act, 1981. The Preamble of the Act specifically states that it has been enacted to take appropriate steps for the prevention of any confined space as is referred in sub-section (1), until all particiable measures have been taken to remove any gas, fume, vapour or dust, which be presented so as to bring its level within the permissible limits and to prevent any ingress of such gas, fume, vapour or dust and unless

(a) a certificate in writing has been given by a competent person, based on a test carried out by himself that the space is reasonably free from dangerous gas, fume, vapour or dust; or
(b) such person is wearing suitable breathing apparatus and a belt securely attached to a rope, the free-end of which is held by a person out side the confined space.

Keeping in view the importance of air quality, Himachal Pradesh Environment Protection and Pollution Control Board has taken various matter concerning to the improvement of the quality of air and prevention, control of air pollution. The monitoring of Ambient Air Quality was started in 1986-87 under the National Ambient Air Quality Monitoring (NAAQM) Programme with the objective to find the current status of pollution and to study the trends as a result of increasing industrialization. The general objectives of the programme are:

(a) To evaluate the general air quality conditions in the city and to provide the basis for analyzing long term trends of pollution concentrations.
(b) To provide the data for subsequent development of air quality standards and pollution prevention and control programme for the city.

Ambient Air Quality Standards

On the basis of land-use pattern air quality standards has been classified for the following three categories:

(a) Industrial and Mixed use Areas.
(b) Residential and Rural areas.
(c) Sensitive areas.

Table 3.1 provides an effective idea regarding the general quality conditions of air in Himachal Pradesh and Ambient Air Quality Standards at National Level.

In Himachal Pradesh Air Quality is being monitored at four locations namely, Shimla, Paranoid, Ponta Sahib and Damsel for SPM, SO_2 and Kn_{ox} under NAAQM project sponsored by Central Pollution Control Board.

NAAQM Network

Shimla is an important hill station and has remained Summer Capital of India during British regime. In 1972 it became the capital of Himachal Pradesh State. Large number of tourist visits the city in summer and other festivals time. The Shimla is located at intersection of 30° 31' North latitude and 77° 21' East longitudes. The monitoring at Shimla is based on two stations. Tables 3.2 and 3.3 provide the idea of air quality in the capital.

Tables 3.2 and 3.3 reveal that the average mean values of gases SO_2 and NO_x at both stations at Shimla are observed below the maximum permissible limits. However, the peak values of SO_2 and NO_x as high as 33.5 and 61.25 ug/m^3 in the month of April and May 1998 for Station No. 1, respectively. In case of SPM the peak values of SPM is absorbed at highest in April at Station No. 1.

Air quality of Parwanoo town is monitored by the two different locations. Tables 3.4 and 3.5 provide the idea of air quality in Parwanoo.

TABLE 3.1: National Ambient Air Quality Standards

Pollutant	Time weighted average	Concentration in ambient air			
		Industrial area	Residential, rural and other area	Sensitive	Method of measurement
1	2	3	4	5	6
Sulphur Dioxide (SO_2)	Annual average	80 $\mu g/m^3$	60 $\mu g/m^3$	15 $\mu g/m^3$	– Improved West and Greek method – Ultraviolet Fluorescence
	24 hours**	120 $\mu g/m^3$	80 $\mu g/m^3$	30 $\mu g/m^3$	
Oxides of Nitrogen (NO_2)	Annual average	80 $\mu g/m^3$	60 $\mu g/m^3$	15 $\mu g/m^3$	– Jacab and Hochhwiser (Na-Arsenite) method
	24 hours**	120 $\mu g/m^3$	80 $\mu g/m^3$	30 $\mu g/m^3$	– Gas-Phase Chemilusence
Suspended Particulate Master (SPM)	Annual average*	360 $\mu g/m^3$	140 $\mu g/m^3$	70 $\mu g/m^3$	– High Volume Sampling – [Average flow rate not less than 1.1 m^3 minute]
	24 hours**	500 $\mu g/m^3$	200 $\mu g/m^3$	100 $\mu g/m^3$	
	Annual average*	120 $\mu g/m^3$	60 $\mu g/m^3$	50 $\mu g/m^3$	– Respirable particulate master sampler
	24 hours**	150 $\mu g/m^3$	100 $\mu g/m^3$	75 $\mu g/m^3$	
Lead (Pb)	Annual average*	1.0 $\mu g/m^3$	0.75 $\mu g/m^3$	0.50 $\mu g/m^3$	– AAS method after sampling using EPM 2000 or equivalent filter paper
	24 hours**	1.5 $\mu g/m^3$	1.00 $\mu g/m^3$	0.75 $\mu g/m^3$	
Carbon Monoxides	8 hours*	5.0 mg/m^3	2.0 mg/m^3	1.0 mg/m^3	– Non Dispers, infrared spectroscopy
	1 hour	10.0 mg/m^3	4.0 mg/m^3	4.0 mg/m^3	

Source: Annual Reports, HPPCB.

TABLE 3.2: Ambient Air Quality Of Shimla (Station No. 1)

Months	SO_2		Kn_{ox}		SPM	
	M. Agg.	Peak	M. Avg.	Peak	M. Avg.	Peak
April, 98	1.44	2.62	5.31	9.58	354.47	1398.86
May, 98	1.58	3.42	5.39	9.58	76.54	352.71
June, 98	1.58	4.85	4.95	12.35	84.07	336.33
July, 98	1.42	2.17	4.35	7.08	62.47	194.89
August, 98	1.11	1.79	3.78	7.22	50.20	208.04
Sept., 98	1.36	3.57	3.97	9.06	6.95	21.67
Oct., 98	1.50	5.13	4.44	11.56	23.69	94.03
Nov., 98	4.63	10.83	1.53	4.02	37.68	555.71
Dec., 98	1.59	2.97	9.04	4.21	28.38	53.62
January 99	1.22	1.61	3.86	6.18	22.23	48.13
Feb., 99	1.41	2.31	2.85	4.79	36.30	63.29
March, 99	1.79	4.24	5.95	15.83	9.93	32.34

Source: Annual Report 1998-1999, HPCB.

TABLE 3.3: Ambient Air Quality Of Shimla (Station No. 2)

Months	SO_2		NO_x		SPM	
	M. Agg.	Peak	M. Avg.	Peak	M. Avg.	Peak
April, 98	3.59	12.5	15.56	61.25	490.26	306.54
May, 98	4.82	33.5	14.66	55.83	156.67	750.57
June, 98	4.55	7.14	13.05	35.83	166.24	583.95
July, 98	3.88	8.71	14.06	30.00	90.62	236.93
August, 98	3.48	11.07	12.00	37.33	90.54	358.37
Sept., 98	3.48	11.26	13.20	40.33	10.78	20.23
Oct., 98	3.61	10.72	12.94	37.92	74.35	614.69
Nov., 98	3.59	10.94	12.74	17.60	72.21	218.37
Dec., 98	3.30	4.73	8.88	7.40	91.75	143.33
January 99	3.48	5.48	14.55	19.35	91.84	181.49
Feb., 99	3.83	5.29	10.35	13.31	104.48	143.01
March, 99	3.48	5.54	14.32	21.33	13.29	20.79

Source: Annual Report 1998-1999, HPCB.

TABLE 3.4: Ambient Air Quality of Parwanoo (Station No. 1)

Months	SO_2		NO_x		SPM	
	M. Agg.	Peak	M. Avg.	Peak	M. Avg.	Peak
April, 98	3.59	12.5	15.56	61.25	490.26	306.54
April, 98	2.0	2.5	10.14	21.80	128.02	566.80
May, 98	2.0	2.5	7.24	16.43	132.10	468.60
June, 98	2.0	2.5	7.49	15.93	136.13	373.65
July, 98	2.0	2.5	7.36	15.45	72.67	287.09
August, 98	2.0	2.5	6.29	23.03	84.95	237.87
Sept., 98	2.0	2.5	10.97	33.68	114.25	475.26
Oct., 98	2.0	2.5	9.47	24.90	91.31	351.28
Nov., 98	2.0	2.5	10.58	34.36	119.75	218.76
Dec., 98	2.0	2.5	11.06	29.13	174.42	327.98
January 99	2.0	2.5	9.65	16.68	191.02	566.26
Feb., 99	2.0	2.5	14.99	59.75	135.47	437.50
March, 99	2.0	2.5	14.33	30.63	187.11	599.68

Source: Annual Report 1998-1999, HPCB.

TABLE 3.5: Ambient Air Quality of Parwanoo (Station No. 2)

Months	SO_2		NO_x		SPM	
	M. Agg.	Peak	M. Avg.	Peak	M. Avg.	Peak
April, 98	2.0	2.0	14.38	37.63	280.28	484.99
May, 98	2.0	2.0	8.13	24.40	269.27	532.72
June, 98	2.0	2.5	8.95	14.00	190.15	357.66
July, 98	2.0	2.0	7.55	15.27	136.74	299.12
August, 98	2.0	2.0	6.17	13.28	130.85	312.69
Sept., 98	2.0	2.0	11.05	11.90	132.23	232.51
Oct., 98	2.0	2.0	10.21	36.10	224.76	595.58
Nov., 98	2.0	2.0	15.52	27.39	363.31	945.68
Dec., 98	2.0	2.0	12.15	23.65	483.23	1763.61
January 99	2.0	2.0	11.03	17.68	274.36	878.33
Feb., 99	2.0	2.0	13.66	24.90	239.53	746.55
March, 99	2.0	2.0	16.55	27.39	234.02	610.88

Source: Annual Report 1998-1999, HPCB.

As is evident from the tables that at Station No. 1 and 2 in Parwanoo the air quality with respect to SO_2 concentration is very good. The analysis reveals that throughout the year the levels of the SO_2 remained below 3 ug/m^3. The high levels of NO_x observed especially during April, 1998, October, 1998, Novembver,1998 and February, 1999 for station No. 2 and 1 respectively showing high traffic intensity during apple session. Contributions from industrial sources are also evident from the observations made at Station No. 2, High values of SPM have been recorded during the dry season. From the above observations, it can be concluded that quality of air is comparatively poor at Station No. 2 in comparison to Station No. 1, the reason for which is more industrial and vehicular activities in the area.

Water Pollution: The Role of Board

The major sources of pollution of our natural water are the discharge of wastes from industry and human settlements. The two major causes of water pollution are:

(a) discharge of all city wastes; and
(b) discharge of industrial effluents into the rivers.

The pollution of water resources is a consequence of:

- Natural processes: erosion, volcanic activities, biological processes and human activities.
- Increasing erosion owing to deforestation, wrong cultivation practices and urbanization.
- Washing of agrochemicals from agricultural and silvicultural production.
- Accident during the transport of fuel and other chemicals.
- Disposal of gaseous, liquid and solid wastes from industry, thermal and nuclear power generation, agricultural, dwelling areas, etc.
- Subsequent bleaching of wastes deposited on the surface, under the ground of in water.
- Infiltration of polluted water from or to ground water resources, etc.[53]

With a view to carrying out its functions properly, the HPCB has given several powers under the Water (Prevention and Control of Pollution) Act, 1974. These include;

(i) to obtain information and conduct survey of any area and gauge and keep record of the flow and other characteristics of any stream or well in the area;
(ii) to take samples of water, trade or any other effluent or of any sewage or effluents for the purpose of making analysis;
(iii) to enter and inspect any premises for the purpose of performing its functions under the Act and to see whether direction of the Board are carried out, and to examine any plant, etc. and records of the establishment;
(iv) to prohibit disposal of effluent in the streams and wells;
(v) to restrict new outlets, discharge for sewage and industrial effluents.

Legal Regulation of Water Pollution

The United Nations has repeatedly expressed deep anxiety over the ceaseless pollution all over the world and innumerable problems it creates. Under the auspices of the United Nations Conference on Human Environment was held at Stockholm, which laid down the principles and action plan for controlling and regulating human environment and institutional and financial arrangements for that purpose. The General Assembly of UN also passed a resolution on 15th December 1972 emphasizing co-operation between the States in the field of conservation of human environment.

India is one of few countries of the world that have made specific reference in the constitution to the need for environmental protection and improvement. The most comprehensive legislation in India for the prevention and control of water pollution are the following:

(i) The Water (Prevention and Control of Pollution) Act, 1974.
(ii) The Water (Prevention and Control of Pollution) Amended Act, 1978.

(iii) The water (Prevention and Control of Pollution) Cess. Act, 1977.
(iv) The Environment Protection Act, 1986.

River Monitoring

Assessment of the status of water quality of the natural water bodies is one of the most important activities of HP Pollution Control Board. Water quality data not only helps to ascertain the nature and extent of the requirement for pollution control measures but also indicates the impact of water quality of any control measures taken. The water quality monitoring of major rivers of the country is being sponsored by Central Pollution Control Board (CPCB) under a National Programme called Monitoring of National Aquatic Resources (Minerals). In Himachal Pradesh it is being carried out quarterly i.e. in the month of March, June, September and December. In all 23 points have been selected on major rivers Satluj, Beas, Ravi and their tributaries and 22 parameters of each sample are being analysed with includes the physiochemical and bacteriological contents. The results are shown in Table 3.6.

Sample Parameters

The following are the various parameters which are analysed on the major rivers Sutlej, Beas and Ravi and their tributaries.

Physical Parameters

pH, Temperature, colour, turbidity, conductivity.

Mineral Constituents

(i) Alkalinity, sulphate, chloride.
(ii) Hardness, Sodium.

Indicator of Organic Pollution

(i) Dissolved Oxygen (DO)
(ii) Biochemical Oxygen Demand (BOD)
(iii) Nitrogen (TKN, Nitrites).

TABLE 3.6: Primary Water Quality Criteria

Designated Base Use	Class of Water	Criteria
Drinking water source without conventional treatment but after disinfections.	A	1. Total Coliform organised MPN/100 ml. shall be 50 or less. 2. pH between 6.5 and 8.5. 3. Dissolved Oxygen 6 mg/l or more. 4. Biochemical Oxygen Demand 5 days 20°C 2 mg/l or less
Outdoor bathing (Organised)	B	1. Total Coliform organised MPN/100 ml. shall be 500 or less 2. pH between 6.5 and 8.5 3. Dissolved Oxygen 6 mg/l or more 4. Biochemical Oxygen Demand 5 days 20°C 2 mg/l or less
Drinking Water Sources	C	1. Total Coliform organised MPN/100 ml. shall be 5000 or less 2. pH between 6.5 and 9 3. Dissolved Oxygen 4 mg/l or more 4. Biochemical Oxygen Demand 5 days 20°C 3 mg/l or less
Propagation of Wild Life Fisheries	D	1. pH between 6.5 and 9.5

Source: Annual Reports HPCB, Shimla.

Bacteriological Parameters

Total and Facial Coliforms: In addition to centrally sponsored programme the State Board has also started conducting the minority of Water Quality of certain rivers, Khads, Nallahas and Lakes such as Giri River, Markanda River, Sirsa River, Kaushalya River, Sawan Khad, Banner Khad, Jattawala Nallah, Sukhana Nallah, Khaziar Lake, Riwalser Lake, etc. In all 22 points have been selected on above rivers, Khads and Nallahs and monitoring is being carried out along with MINARS programme.

The above programme is being carried out with objectives mentioned below:

(i) Data storage, processing, retrieval and Interpretation.

(ii) General Health of Rivers.
(iii) To compare the existing status of quality of various stretches of rivers with the respective objectives.
(iv) To identify the polluted stretches where immediate action needs to be taken.

The data analysis is being done with specific objective of classification of river water quality suitable to drinking, irrigation and industrial process mentioned in Primary Water Quality Criteria. In case of major rivers on the basis of Primary Water Quality, it is concluded that quality of river falls under "A" category of water with respect pH, DO and BOD. The critical parameter observed total Coliform according to which category of river comes down to "C" category in general. The urban-based affects water quality near town and water resources is required to be treated and disinfected before it used for drinking purposes.

Vehicular Pollution in the State: Role of HPCB

The State Environment Protection and Pollution Control Board is not directly responsible for checking the vehicular pollution. The State Transport Department is the implementing authority for control of vehicular pollution under the Motor Vehicle Act, 1988 and the specification for allowable emission and permissible level of noise are clearly laid down under the Central Motor Vehicles Rules, 1989. However, on the recommendations of the State Board, the Government has notified the emission and noise level standards for both diesel and petrol driven vehicles under the Air (Prevention and Control of Pollution) Act, 1981 also.

The State Board in co-ordination with the State Transport Department has conducted surveys to assess the vehicular emission from time to time and taken steps to create awareness and persuasively induce vehicle owners to rectify their engines to achieve reduction in emissions to desirable levels. Steps for on the spot rectification of petrol engines were also taken by the H.P. State Environment Protection and Pollution Control Board during survey camps, which have now been made a regular feature. The surveys conducted by the Board at Una indicate that 56.7

per cent of vehicles (Diesel Driven) monitored exceeds the prescribed limits and for petrol driven 35.6 per cent of the vehicles exceeds the prescribed limit.

The use of pressure horn is prohibited under the provision of Motor Vehicles Act, 1988 as amended from time to time. The said Act and Central Motor Vehicles Rules, 1989 also provided for use of silencers is now onwards being included in all future camps of H.P. State Pollution Control Board. The following action taken for vehicular emission control:

(1) ***Authorization of Workshop and Petrol Pumps:*** H.P. State Pollution Control Board has initiated steps for vehicular emission check, although the response is not encouraging.

(2) ***Public Awareness Campaign:*** The State Board has taken up steps in this regard by way of awareness campaigns on the eve of World Environment Day, Pollution Prevention Week and during routine vehicular monitoring surveys.

(3) ***Notification of Vehicular Monitoring Equipments:*** The Board has already recommended to State Transport Authority for notification of following vehicular monitoring equipment:

(i) 'Heritage'	Smoke meter
(ii) HP	-do-
(iii) AVL	-do-
(iv) 'Ricken'	CO/HC Analyser

(4) ***Notice to Indian Oil Corporation:*** Indian Oil Corporation has been advised to provide whether winter grade diesel during winter period all over the State particularly at HRTC bulk depots. As per the directions of the State Pollution Control Board, the HRTC has already started taking steps towards this concept.

(5) ***Installation of Turbo-Charges and catalytic converters to reduce the vehicular emission:*** The matter has already been taken up with the HRTC for making provisions as above in a phased manner to reduce the vehicular emission.

(6) ***Steps taken by HRTC:*** Fleet renewal fleet maintenance, turbo charge winter grade diesel fuel additives, drivers training pollution check, etc.

State Road Transport Corporation in Himachal Pradesh is working or governed by Motor Vehicles Act, Motor Transport Act in addition to various other labour and taxation laws. These Acts allow considerable scope of corporation to function on commercial lines and enables them to take and implement decisions speedily without being tied down to rigid procedure.

Pollution Control—Surveillance and Monitoring

The Himachal Pradesh Environments Protection and Pollution Control Board is working within the ambit of the functions bestowed on it under Section 17 of the Water (Prevention and Control of Pollution) Act, 1974 and the Air (Prevention and Control of Pollution) Act, 1981 ensures sustainable development with due regard to the environment protection and conservation.

Consent to establish is granted to the industry by the State Board after evaluation of the potential environmental pollution and after the examination of the engineering design and details of the systems proposed for the controlling the pollution. The conditions consistent to control requirements are incorporated in consent to establish. These conditions are reviewed in terms of their compliance and 'Consent to Establish' is 'converted to operate' after ensuring that the engineering system for control of water and air pollution are fully implemented. The 'Consent to Operate' is usually valid for one year, which is also granted subject to the condition that the control systems shall be so operated, and maintain as to ensure compliance to the standards prescribed for emission and effluents as the case may be. The Status of consents dealt with and feel realized during the year 1998-99 is given in Table 3.7.

Consent and Cess Management at a Glance (1998-99)

The operational and qualitative efficiency of the pollution control derives installed in different industries largely on regular surveillance and monitoring of the pollution control equipment.

This activity is presently being conducted by a network of 10 Regional Offices of the Board headed by Environmental Engineers and Assistant Environmental Engineers. During the year 1998-99,

TABLE 3.7: Consent and Cess Management at a Glance (1998-99)

Particulars	Granted during the year (1998-99)		Reused during the year (1998-99)		Cumulative as on 31.03.99	
	At HQ	At ROS	At HQ	At ROS	At HQ	At ROS
1. Consent to Establish						
(a) Water Act, 1974	42	148	2	–	1381	321
(b) Air Act, 1981	42	99	–	–	1220	220
(c) Non-Polluting	–	123	–	–	50	179
2. Consent to Operate						
(a) Water Act, 1974	72	104	–	–	1047	285
(b) Air Act, 1981	73	93	–	–	856	189
(c) Non-Polluting	–	34	–	–	–	57
3. Renewal of Consent						
(a) Water Act, 1974	136	609	–	–	–	–
(b) Air Act, 1981	180	369	–	–	–	–
4. Consent Fees (in Rs.)			84,32,620.00			
5. Cess under Water Cess Act, 1977 (in Rs.)	Assessment 11,18,663.00			Realization 11,68,754.00		
6. (I) Samples of industrial wastes, solid wastes, stack/dust emissions, ground and surface water, other than those under MINARS and NAAQM, collected during the year	No. of Samples Collected					
	Water/Effluents 1077		Air/Emission 393		Solid Wastes 13	
7. Evaluation and verification of Environment Adult Reports		No. Received 32		No. Evaluated/Verified 32		
8. Public Complaints representations	No. Received		104	–	104	
	No. attended and action taken		104	–	104	
9. (i) Number of injunctions issued U/S33-A and 31A of Water and Air Acts respectively			16	Power not delegated to RO's	16	
(ii) Number actually implemented on site			16		16	

Source: Annual Report, HPPCB.

the surveillance and monitoring was carried out and the salient achievements in the context are presented below:

(i)	Number of Water Pollution Control System (Cumulative)	828
(ii)	Number of Air Pollution Control System (Cummulative)	807
(iii)	Number of Inspections conducted in 1998-99	3642
(iv)	Number of Samples of water, waste water and emission including ambient air in 1998-99	1477
(v)	Environmental Audit Statements compiled and verified	32

Source: HPCB, Shimla.

As a result of surveillance and monitoring activities, constant pressure is maintained on the polluting industries for operation and maintenance of the pollution control equipment. During the year 145 new pollution control systems were got installed in the new industries to whom consents to operate were granted during the year. Similarly, improvements in the already existing control systems in respect of 16 industries were got incorporated. In addition exercising regular checks ensured smooth functioning of the pollution control systems installed in the existing industries. Apart from the inspections and sampling of the pollution control devices, the following activities were also conducted during the year to promote awareness and provide engineering inputs to the entrepreneurs at field level:

- Introduction of the concept of Joint Industrial Planning and Management in Baddi—Barotiwala area.
- Introduction of Self Regulatory order in the industries for involvement of the entrepreneurs in environmental programmes.
- Introduction of awards in Environmental Excellence for the industries, local bodies and NGO's doing pioneering work in the protection of environment.
- Published a document titled "Guidelines for the Entrepreneurs on Environmental Clearances" was released by the Hon'ble Chief Ministry of Himachal Pradesh.
- Classification of industrial and developmental projects in "Red", "Orange" and "Green" categories according to pollution potential of a project.

- Evolution and formulation of Environmental Management Plan for de-silting operations of the BSL Project for disposal of silt in 94 environmentally sound manner to solve the endemic problems of the people of the Balh valley.
- Field level surveillance for management of hazardous wastes.
- Auto-exhaust monitoring by the Regional Engineers in co-ordination with State Transport Authority.
- Interaction meets at field level for making improvements in control systems.
- Revival of issue of cess on hydel power with Government of India and defended the petitions related thereto in the High Court of Himachal Pradesh.
- Pepped a documentary title "How Clean is Hydel Generation" highlighting the adverse impacts of dams and hydel projects.
- Delegation of powers to Regional Officers so as to introduce transparency and accountability in the system.
- Mining activities integrated in the comprehensive consent mechanism for better environmental management in mining sector.
- Integrating the concept of Environmental Management in all major public works.
- Formulation of techno-economic pollution control systems for Katha and Resin and Turpentine units in small sector.
- Environmental Status Surveys undertaken for Mehatpur, Paonta Sahib, Parwanoo, Baddi, Barotiwala and Kala Amb areas and action initiated for restoration and enhancement of water quality in these areas.
- Projects on Environmental Auditing and formation of Environmental squad prepared and submitted to the Central Pollution Control Board for funding.

Management of Hazardous Chemicals and Bio-Medical Wastes

Under the Environment (Protection) Act, 1986 the Ministry of Environment and Forests (GOI) have notified the following Rules for the management of pollution due to hazardous chemical and wastes.

1. Manufacturer, Storage and Import of Hazardous Chemicals Rule, 1989.
2. Manufacture, Storage and Import of Hazardous Chemicals Rule, 1989.
3. Rules of Manufacture, Use, Import, Export and Storage of Hazardous Micro-Organism, Genetically Engineered Organisms or Cells.
4. The Public Liability Insurance Act, 1991.
5. The Bio-Medical Waste (Management and Handling) Rules, 1998.

Under the provision of above Rules the Board has been entrusted with specific responsibility for the implementation of various sections of the Rules. Under the Manufacture, Storage and Import of Hazardous Chemical Rules, 1989, the Board has identified more than 150 units using the Hazardous Chemicals as a part of consent management for establishing and operating the industrial units in the State. Such hazardous installations have been persuaded to prepare On-Site Emergency Plan and to have the facilities installed for meeting emergencies in case of accidents.

For effective implementation of the Public Liability Insurance Act, the Board has been successful in getting 11 units take the insurance policies to pay immediately and to cover the damage to life and property in case of any accident.

The Board has identified 116 units responsible for generating waste falling into the various categories of Hazardous Waste listed in Schedule 1 under the Hazardous Waste (Management and Handling) Rules, 1989. All such units have been asked to obtain the authorization for on site secured storage of waste. The Board has granted the authorization to 71 units. Further, for the effective implementation of the Hazardous Waste (Management and Handling) Rules, 1989, the Ministry of Environment and Forests, Government of India has entrusted the task of Environmental Impact Study for Identification of Hazardous Waste Disposal site for District Solan and Sirmour. The Boar has completed the EIA study for the District Solan and has also identified the suitable site for disposal of Hazardous Waste near Baddi in Nalagarh Tehsil. Based on the EIA study, layout plan and estimate are being prepared for developing the site and installation of treatment facilities.

The Ministry of Environment and Forests, Government of India notified the Bio-Medical Waste (Management and Handling) Rules, 1998 under Section 6, 8 and 25 of the Environment (Protection Act, 1987 on 20th July 1998. The Government of Himachal Pradesh notified the H.P. State Pollution Control Board as Prescribed Authority for the implementation of the Bio-Medical Waste (Management and Handling) Rules, 1998, vide Notification No. EDN/ST&E/3/-6/98 dated November 10,1998. The Board played the proactive role by organising a State Level Seminar followed by 11 workshops in 8 districts on Management Bio-Medical Waste, distributed the copies of the Bio-Medical Waste (Management and Handling) Rules, 1998 to all concerned departments for wide publicity).

Solid Waste Disposal

Urban solid waste, generated from various activities, is another major source of pollution. None of the towns have any proper treatment facility for its disposal like incinerators, etc. River banks or tributary banks are being used for its disposal in open, which ultimately affects the river water quality. Large heaps of solid waste on the banks is a common site. During rainy season, this waste washes away into the river and its tributaries. In Manali town, a total of 23 m^3/day of solid waste is generated/collected. The present disposal site is near Bombay Kothi in open on the right bank of the river and NAC Manali is also disposing the garbage on the bank of 'Priny Nallah'. At Kullu, 22 m^3/day of garbage is collected and disposal by trucks, in an open space near Lanka Bazar on the right bank of the 'River Beas'. In Mandi town, there is around 17 m^3/day solid waste (garbage), Mode of disposal is by tractors to an open space on the bank of 'Suketi Khad' and bank of river Beas at Khaliar.

It is recommended to have a provision of incinerators, one at each town for disposal of the solid waste. Composting facilities shall also be installed for treatment of biodegradable solid waste.

The estimated cost shall be around Rs.60 lakh for each set of solid waste disposal system excluding assistance of Rs.20 lakh from Government of India in each case.

	(Rs. in lakhs)
Total Cost Estimate for providing complete system for three towns	180.00
@ Rs.60 lakh/each	180.00

Provision For Crematoria

Although, there exists crematories in each of these towns, like in Mandi, there are six crematoria along the bank of river Beas, in Kullu, there exists three Nos. on the bank of the river i.e., at Bhutnath temple, Lakkar Bazar and Gandhi Nagar and none of these crematories have been designed properly and at least there needs on planned crematoria in each of these towns.

The estimated cost provisions for providing one crematoria at each of these three towns shall be as under:

Total cost estimate for 3 Town providing one crematoria in each town	Rs.60.00
@ Rs. 20 lakhs each	Rs.60.00

Development of River Bank

To prevent soil erosion and open defecating of the river banks, it is necessary to develop these river banks adjoining these towns into grasslands/green parks, Bathing ghats, embankment, etc. It has also become essential in view of recent Hon'ble Court Orders banning all the construction activities on the river banks in state.

The components for developing these river banks into grass lands/parks, etc. shall start initially with the preparation of development plans including survey work, preparation of draft/final plans. The total estimated budget for the development of river banks, etc. shall be around Rs.50 lakh/town.

Beas Action Plan

The Ganga Project Directorate (GPD) identified the River Beas in Himachal Pradesh as polluted stretch on the basis of MINARS data sent to Central Pollution Control Board by H.P. State Pollution Control Board. On the direction of GPD the Central Pollution Control Board assigned the work of detail survey of polluted stretches of river Beas in H.P. to the Board for its inclusion in National River Action Plan for restoration of water quality. On the basis of field survey and study, the Board prepared the Beas Action Plan the findings and recommendations for undertaking restoration work as follows.

For rational formulation of any pollution control programme a complete knowledge on nature, source and quantum of pollution load which a given water body is subjected to, is required to, is required. The short term study identifies the following critical areas for detailed study and preparation of pollution control scheme.

(a) Based on the present study, the towns situated on the river banks i.e. Manali, Kullu, Bhunter, Pandoh, Mandi, Nadoun and Dehra Gopipur has a direct impact on water quality of river Beas provided with sewerage system and sewage treatment facility in the first phase. In addition town having discharge of sewage into the near by nallah which also has impact on the river Beas should also be provided with sewerage system and sewage treatment facilities in the second phase. These towns are Sunder Nagar, Joginder Nagar, Sarkaghat, Baijnath, Paprola, Palampur, Hamirpur, Yole Cantt, Nagrota Bhagwan, Kangra and Dharamshala.

(b) Based on the data collected under MINARS Programme since 1983 the classification of river water quality shows the quality of river Beas at upstream of Manali has deteriorated to class 'B' from class 'A' and needs to be restored. Similarly the classification at down stream area shows class 'C' quality of the river with Total and Faecal Coliform as the critical parameters. Immediate steps are required to check the sewage pollution and to ensure safe supply of drinking water by ensuring the proper disinfections.

(c) The industrial unit M/S Phementa Ferma Biodil Ltd. at Village Takoli in District Mandi also shows its impact on the river water quality specifically in terms of BOD. The unit should have more efficient effluent treatment measures and the possibility of using the effluent for irrigation purpose should be worked out. Steps are also required to be taken for prescribing more stringent standards.

(d) At all urban centre, the garbage is dumped in scattered low lying areas, which ultimately finds its way to the river. Necessary steps are required to be taken for proper collection and disposal of the garbage.

(e) The Pandoh dam diverts the entire river water from its original course thus no water is available for dilution at immediately downstream of the reservoir. Due to this the discharge from sewage treatment plant at Pandoh colony highly pollutes the stretch, the plant not only needs better maintenance and operational efficiency but also zero discharge technology to be applied. The direct discharge of sewage from Police BTN colony needs to be diverted to the sewage treatment plant.

(f) The river Beas has very high potential for hydropower generation and many hydel power plants are in the pipeline. Since construction of Dam not only alters the ecology of the flowing water but also reduces the dilution and dispersion capacity of pollutants in the down stream areas. Thus all proposed hydel projects should be subjected to the critical environmental impact analysis and migration measures incorporated at the Planning stage.

(g) Intensive horticultural activities are being practiced in the basin specialty in upstream area of the Pandoh reservoir. This involves the extensive use of insecticides and pesticide, which are not easily biodegradable and gets bio accumulated. The problem needs to be studied in greater detail.

(h) The concentration of sodium chloride has been increasing very rapidly downstream of the Mandi due to salt mining activities which may have detrimental effects on aquatic flora and fauna and water used for irrigation purpose. Detailed study is required for combating the problem and implementing necessary measures.

(i) All critical areas identified during this study needs to be monitored frequently and extensively under already established MINARS Programme. Several additional monitoring points need to be incorporated in the programme.

(j) Comparative analysis of data of four seasons monitored under MINARS Programme shows the water quality more deteriorated in respect of all the parameters in the month of September.

Wetland Studies: Water Quality Monitoring of Pong Wetland

Under the management and conservation of wetlands, H.P. State Environment Protection and Pollution Control Board has been entrusted to conduct water quality monitoring of Pong Dam Reservoir. Under the proposal, both surface and deep-water quality monitoring of this wetland is to be conducted quarterly for a year and quality parameter, bacteriological parameters and for the metals, covering all four seasons. The monitoring and analysis under the project is under progress.

Environmental Planning Through Zoning Atlas

The environmental planning programme stared in early 1995 at the State Pollution Control Board in co-ordination with Central Pollution Control Board and technical assistance/advisory services from German Agency for Technical Co-operation (GTZ). In the first phase, District Solan was taken up for preparation of the Zoning Atlas. Based on the experience gained in the Pilot Phase and encouraged by the positive response from all concerned, the study was extended for three more Districts viz. Sirmour, Una and Bilaspur. The Ministry of Environment and Forests (MOEF), Government of India is providing funds for the Zoning Atlas Programme, which is for five years starting from 1997-98 to 2001-02, under the World Bank Environmental Management Capacity Building Project. The programme includes developing of infrastructural facilities in the State Pollution Control Board for taking up environmental planning tasks.

The Zoning Atlas prepared for district Solan,[54] classifies and does zonation of the environment of the district and presents the pollution receiving potential of various sites/zones in the district and the possible alternate sites for industrial development. In addition to streamlining the decision making process, it has several benefits some of which are briefed below:

(a) It provides a ready reckoner for best suitable site and relevant environmental information;
(b) Makes decision-making process simpler, faster, realistic, transparent and reliable;
(c) Provides a basis for incorporating environmental aspects into physical (land-use) planning process, which is lacking in this country;
(d) Helps in planning, cost-effective pollution control measures and programmes;
(e) Helps to check additional pollution in the areas already over stressed with pollution;
(f) Ensures that pollution potential of an industry is made compatible with the local conditions of the site;
(g) Helps an entrepreneur to identify the most suitable industrial site, matching both environmental and economic considerations;
(h) The regulatory authority can plan better control and monitoring programmes;
(i) The public can participate in the decision-making process on the type of industrial development in their neighbourhood;
(j) Atlas helps to achieve the goals of sustainable development.

Impact of Mining Activities

Under the Ministry of Environment and Forests, Government of

India funded project, studies were initiated to know the impact of mining on aquifers in Himachal Pradesh. In Himachal Pradesh mining activity is concentrated in limestone beating belts of Simons district namely—Satun-Kamraoo Shilla, Tilordhar, Bhoot-mari and Naura. Besides limestones mining is confirmed to a small area near Solan where the mining leases of limestone are being worked. The HPCB took up the studies in district Sirmour to study the impact of mining on aquifers with the help of samples, collected from the limestone mining areas.

Urban Solid Waste Management

With rapid growth of urban areas due to population explosion and industrial revolution, the problem of garbage collection and disposal has assumed importance and has drawn the attention of civic authorities and government to standardize the system to make it applicable at the National level. Solid wastes arise in association with almost every activity of man. The problem of urban solid waste disposal has become very acute in large cities because of the limited disposal facilities. As a result, the solid wastes are dumped in a haphazard manner in various parts of the city causing thereby not only the environmental problems but also serious health hazards. The composition and properties of these wastes reflect the diversity of man's action. Characterizations of waste are usually associated with broad description of the sources of waste.

H.P. State Pollution Control Board has conducted a detailed survey of Urban Solid Waste Management in various towns including Shimla, Mandi, Dharamshala, Chamba, Solan and Nalagarh. Following action point for management of municipal solid waste have been recommended.

Collection and Segregation

- House-to-house collection of garbage should be practiced either by municipal agencies through their own efforts or through a contractual arrangement/voluntary organisations (N.G.O.'s) invariably encourage public participation in the collection of garbage.

- Encourage segregation of garbage at the household level itself for that distinctly marked bags should be provided. Biodegradable waste may be processed and utilized as compost. Non-biodegradable and recyclable waste should be routed through organized waste-pickers. Organized waste-pickers are preferred to be rag-pickers.
- Adopt suitable means of collection of waste generated by traders of fruits, vegetables, fast-food corners, etc.
- Similarly, slaughterhouse waste should be properly regulated and the solid waste they generate should be prevented from mixing with community garbage.
- Hospital and other infectious waste should not be allowed to be dumped in community bins. Biomedical wastes should be disposed off in consonance with the standards and guidelines laid down under the Biomedical Rules.

Storage of Waste

- An adequate number of bins of appropriate size, should be placed in residential localities. It is advisable to replace conventional concrete/ brick bins and masonry structures with modern, scientifically designed ones. Facilities like dumper placers to suit transport should be preferred.
- Community bins should be well maintained and regularly inspect by the staff. It is the civic authorities responsibility to take measures to check the entry of stray animals in the vicinity of such bins and inside receptacle. In any case, stray animals scouring community bins for their food should be curtailed. The staff assigned field duty should visit the areas under their charge regularly and ensure that the waste receptacles remain tidy and well maintained. Spillage of garbage, entry of stray animals, unorganized rag-picking should be prohibited. Alongside, the civic authorities should remain vigilant and see to it that the public do not dispose garbage at unidentified/non-designated places. Penalizing violators will act as a deterrent.
- Collection of waste in 'open sites' should be prohibited.

Movable bins should be kept for collection of wastes at sites for social functions, like marriages.

- Manual handling/lifting of waste should be prohibited; multiple handling of waste should be avoided. If unavoidable, gloves and masks should be provided to the Safai Karamchari.
- Provide bins in commercial areas as well as official complexes. Market associations should be involved in the upkeep of their civic activities. Roping in the market associations will also lead to the participation of the local business community and also help in penalizing offenders, in forms of levying fines.

Transportation of Waste

- The daily lifting of garbage from all designated waste receptacles is a must. Also ensure priority to areas receiving large quantities. Such areas need to be attended at least twice a day. The task of lifting garbage may be completed latest by 9 o'clock.
- For smooth and easy collection of garbage from narrow, congested areas and collection of garbage from the areas where vehicle approach is not possible should be done through chutes/any other suitable methods.
- Vehicles used for transportation of municipal waste should be covered while in operation so that garbage is not exposed during transit. The civic authorities should explore the possibilities of getting vehicles fabricated and manufactured with these requirements in mind. Of course, the size of the vehicle could vary according to requirement.
- Vehicles earmarked for garbage transportation should not be diverted for other assignments. Privatization of municipal waste transport may be attempted.
- Discourage manual loading of garbage on to the collecting vehicles. Introduce mechanical means to replace manpower for the purpose. The movable bins, which can be directly lifted on vehicles, should be preferred. Vehicles similar to dumper placer mechanism should be preferred.

- Provide adequate maintenance facilities for the preventive and routine maintenance of vehicles.

Processing of Waste

- There are various options to process biodegradable wastes. Broadly, biodegradable wastes can be either composted or subjected to energy recovery. For such purpose, participation of private entrepreneurs may be encouraged. Waste from vegetable and fruit markets should be separately processed by biological means instead land-fill sites.
- Non-biodegradable wastes can either be recycled (wherever and whenever possible) or be disposed of at suitable land-fill sites.
- Municipalities should provide land to recycling units or other units showing interest in waste processing on reasonable terms and may also provide necessary infrastructure.
- The Local Self-Government may consider giving incentives to NGOs/private entrepreneurs for setting up recycling units.

Mass Awareness

- Municipal authority should crate public awareness by using newspapers, pamphlets, TV, radio, hoarding, etc. to disseminate information regarding garbage disposal and generally about municipal solid waste. The area in-charge, representing the local authority, should meet representatives of the Resident Welfare Associations and Market Associations to ensure the municipal solid waste are well managed. Local authority may formulate a scheme involving NGOs, Mahila Mandals/Women organisations and may designate a warden in each zone.
- To keep a strict watch on cleanliness and sanitation at the ward level, ward level committees headed by local representatives may be constituted for a ward or a group of wards depending upon area and local conditions.

Environmental Awareness and Public Participation

On the occasion of the World Environment Day celebrated on June 5th every year, the Board organizes the following activities:

(a) Vehicular Monitoring Camps,
(b) Distribution of Pamphlets and Literature on Vehicular Pollution, Air Pollutants in Your Home, Noise Pollution, distributed to the public and school students.
(c) The Board collaborated with the H.P. Council for Science, Technology and Environment in organising painting, slogans, fancy dress, quiz, plastic bag collection, competition and Shimla Cleanliness Campaign.

During the environment week observed from 2nd to 9th December, to commemorate the anniversary of world's worst industrial disaster at Bhopal on 2nd December, 1984 the Board organized the Vehicular Monitoring Camps.

Advertisement and Publicity

H.P. State Pollution Control Board intensified mass awareness campaign through advertisement and publicity. The advertisements and articles highlighting the activities and achievements of the Board published in the leading national and local newspapers, weekly and quarterly magazines like the Indian Express, Himachal Times, Parwat Ki Gunj, Himachal Darpan, Himachal Era, Danik Himalay Dev, Himalaya Times, etc. The Board also encouraged leading entrepreneurs to put up catchy and colourful hoarding at prime spots encouraging the people on need to protect the environment.

The Board also actively associated with Non-Governmental Organisations, Local Schools, Colleges, Mela Committee etc. for undertaking environmental awareness and upgradation programmes like Chain Poster Competition, Fancy Dress, Dance and Drama Shows etc. The officials of the Board also delivered radio talks and lectures on the subject related to environment and pollution control at National Seminars and prestigious institutions such as

Himachal Institute of Public Administration, H.P. University, Gyan Vigyan Samiti, etc.

Training and Workshops

The H.P. State Environment Protection and Pollution Control Board decided to conduct the training and workshops on the following topics:

(i) *Effluent Treatment Plant Operators Training Programme*

The Board along with Industrial Development Bank of India, and H.P. Directorate of Industries has sponsored the three month long Effluent Treatment Operators Training Programme from 25th March to 29th June, 1996. The Himachal Productivity Council has been assigned the task to conduct the programme which covers the 13 day classroom training followed by 13 day Laboratory Training and two months "On the Job Training." The programme, first of its kind, was launched with twin objectives, first to develop skill of operation of Effluent Treatment Plant amongst the unemployed youth with the assurance of getting employed in private sector. Second, the improvement in efficiency of operation treatment plant by trained personnel shall bring down the pollution level.

The selection of candidates for ETP operators training was made through the advertisement and interview of the candidates, who had educational qualifications upto 10th or 12th standard. The candidates shall be given stipend of Rs.800 to Rs.1200 by the industrial unit for their "On the Job Training" of two months and on successful completion of training they will be employed as trainee ETP operators.

(ii) *Workshop on Vegetable Waste Utilization in Hotels/ Restaurants and Food Processing Industry*

The Board along with Ministry of Non-Conventional Energy Source, New Delhi and the Himachal Productivity Council, Shimla, organized two days workshop on Vegetable Waste Utilisation in Hotels/ Restaurants and Food Processing Industry at Kufri Holiday Resort on September 20-21, 1996. The seminar was attended by the large number of personnel from leading hotels, experts and from Ministry of Non-Conventional Energy Sources, Government of India.

(iii) *Environment Management System ISO-1400*

Two days duration Appreciation-cum-Committee training programme on Environment Management System ISO-1400 was organized jointly by the H.P. State Pollution Control Board, Himachal Productivity Council and Confederation of Indian Industry (CII), New Delhi at Hotel Holiday Home, with a view to create awareness about the Environment Management Systems with special reference to ISO-1400.

(iv) *Workshop on Cleaner Manufacturing Technologies*

As awareness workshop on "Cleaner Manufacturing Technologies: was organized by the H.P. State Pollution Control Board in collaboration with Himachal Productivity Council and National Cleaner Production Centre, New Delhi on 9th April, 1996 at Timber Trail Resort, Parwanoo. 50 Professional/entrepreneurs from all over Himachal participated in the workshop. The workshop focused on the importance of cleaner production for prevention pollution by adopting innovation approach to product design process. Modification, natural substitution, or management practices leading to low or no discharge of pollutants.

(v) *Exhibition-cum-Demonstration of Pollution Control Equipment*

For strengthening the laboratory and monitoring network of the Board and realizing the fast pace of technological developments in the field of Pollution monitoring equipment, the H.P. Pollution Control Board organised exhibition-cum-demonstration of pollution control equipments at its headquarters office and the officials of various organisations attended the show. The university teachers and professionals were also benefited in acquiring the knowledge in field of latest monitoring equipment technologies.

Prosecutions Launched and Convictions Secured for Environmental Pollution Control

The Pollution Control Board has its legal wing consisting of a Law Officer drawn on deputation from Prosecution Department of the State Government an Assistant Law Officer and a Senior Assistant. Apart from this assistance is sought from the standing counsels at High Court and District level. As decided vide 39th Board meeting the fee are paid per norms of legal Aid Services Authority Regulation/Law Department.

The legal wing has been managing/looking after cases on behalf of and against the State Pollution Control Board pending in the different courts in the State of H.P. and outside the state including Supreme Court of India. All kind of assistance is being extended to the standing counsels of the Board from time to time for preparing reply/written statements and to produce evidence/record as and when required in the cases. Besides this, legal notices/directions are drafted under the Pollution Control Acts and Vetted to facilitate the concerned wings of the Boards. The Legal Wing also provides legal assistance, which includes legal opinion/advice to the Regional Officers on the clearance of cases/matters involving legal implications.

Compliance from industry has been sought through persuasive/consultative approach with encouraging results thereby, saving time, cost and effort and legal compliance has increased significantly through this co-operative efforts jointly with the industries. However, with increasing awareness about environment and people's right to clean air and water the total workload has increased on account of increasing incidence of public interest litigation and judicial activism.

For resolution of conflicts and environ-legal action, the Board has resorted to innovative approaches, which include institution of public hearing through mediation of Board officials to arrive at mutual agreed solution. Regular notices are issued to the offenders and as and when cognizance is taken the hearings/opportunity are afforded to them by the Board, rather than immediate resort to filing of cases. The success rate of hearing has been phenomenal and resolutions have been possible in most of the cases. In another significant move the Board has also come out with an offer to free legal aid for public interest litigation in environmental related matters.

Apart from this the legal wing prepared/drafted replies on behalf of the State and filed them in the Supreme Court and High Court in cases involving environmental matters. Also the legal wing prepared draft Air rules under the Air Act. Some of the statistical indicators pertaining to legal wing are given in Table 3.8.

TABLE 3.8: Cases of Environmental Matters in the Courts

Name of Court	No. of pending Cases	Decided	Balance
1. Supreme Court	5	Nil	5
2. High Court Cases/PIL	30	6	24
3. Human Right Commission	3	1	2
4. Lower Courts	13	3 (Favour 2, Against 1)	10
5. Administrative Tribunal	1	Nil	1

Source: HPCB, Shimla

Environmental Training: An Objective

Initial training for environmental specialists has an important concept towards the environmental conservation and development Training for professional including decision-makers and administrators create more professional approach in the organisations. The environmental training programmes specially organisation like Himachal Pradesh State Environment Conservation and Pollution Control Board deals with:

1. Acquire basic understanding of the interrelationships of component and factors of the achievement and the processes that occur in it.

2. Develop desirable values and attitudes, specially concern and responsibility towards the conservation and enhancement of the environment.
3. Acquire and refine skills in identifying, assessing, and solving environmental problems.
4. Develop a sense of urgency in responding to environmental issues and problems and taking action towards their solution.

Keeping in view the above factors, the H.P. State Board is providing training to the employees at both National and International level in following broad sectors:

- Reserve conservation
- Environmental Economics
- Waste water treatment
- Hazardous waste
- Water Quality Management
- Environment Data Collection quality.

Our race for economic development through industrialization at the cost of environment ultimately leads to disaster. The Government of the State has, in recent years, become increasingly conscious of the growing environmental laws and policy issues towards environmental consideration and development in Himachal Pradesh. Special attention is being paid to environment in different plans, policies, programmes and projects, but still unable to control the menace of environmental pollution. So, the problem of environmental degradation is a complex one of which there can be no single solution. Any viable strategy must take into account not only the physical nature of the problem but also human factors involved.

The Himachal Pradesh Environmental Protection and Pollution Control Board is basically an administrative agency having advisory powers. It has no direct legal duty to prosecute the defaulters. It has also no legal sanction to enforce its policies. The Board can only prosecute but can't punish the polluters or prevent them from polluting the environment. If the matter is taken to courts, it takes years together to dispose of a case and menace remains unchecked.

Hence, the Pollution Control Board should be given powers to take a direct action against the defaulter. The Board should be independent with powers to enforce their decisions. These agencies should be manned by experts. Only persons with professional background should be associated with the working of the organisation.

Functioning of the Pollution Control Board: An Appraisal

Strategic Planning and implementation of remedial policies is the only answer to save the deteriorating trend of environment. Therefore, the State Pollution Control Board in Himachal Pradesh committed to the concept of sustainable development with a policy to encourage the growth of industry without damage to environment. Laws were made and laws are being framed, but more important is the proper implementation of these laws to achieve the desired results. Although the Himachal Pradesh Environment Protection and Pollution Control Board is working hard to achieve its objective, but yet the functioning of the Board is not as satisfactory as it should have been. The Board consists of certain nominated persons without having any particular knowledge about environmental conservation and development. The Act prescribes no qualifications and experience for such nominees. Consequently most of the persons so nominated lack interest in pollution control activities and policies. Board has no power to take coercive or punitive measures to take action of some effluent is found to a river or well, but they have no power to prevent apprehended pollution.

Further, the Board feels helpless in taking action against industrialist on violation of law. The Board under Water Act has no power to granting or not granting consent to discharge effluents. But the Board has no legal power to investigate into matter of its consequential impact. The State Environment Protection and Pollution Control Board is not getting cooperation from the industries concerned. The industries hesitate to apply for grant of consent of the Board for installing anti-pollution treatment plants because it may cause financial and technological stress on them. The industries try to ignore the conditions imposed by the Board to improve their house-keeping, treating the trade effluent and discharging them in a appropriate manner on very flimsy grounds, such as absence of technology for treatment, non-availability of land, lack of funds and absence of proper disposal points.

Environmental Pollution is a worldwide phenomenon, therefore, is a need to have co-ordinated administrative structure so that the environmental problems may be taken in a co-ordinated and co-operative way at very wide platform.

4

Participatory Techno-Development

Himachal Pradesh is characterized by diverse climate and large scale variation in physiography. On account of variability in ecological disposition the problems encountered are also varied in nature. Inaccessibility an extreme climate conditions further compound the problems. Science and Technology innovations and scientific knowledge can help in alleviating some of the common problems that come in the way of development. Specific problems of the hill areas require applicable of scientific knowledge and awareness of people regarding latest technological innovations and opportunities, so that they can find solution in tune with the prevailing conditions of these difficulties and far-flung areas of the State. The linkage between the development departments and National Research Institutes require to be strengthened. Prevention of biodiversity and sustainable development compatible with the aspiration of the people living therein is only possible if the plans evolved on scientific links. Science and Technology inputs are also required to be applied to tap untapped resources. The State Council for Science, Technology and Environment was constituted to fulfil this role.

The State Council for Science, Technology and Environment, Himachal Pradesh was established by the Government of Himachal Pradesh during the year 1985 and is a society registered under Registration of Societies Act XXI of 1860.

Scientific and technological contribution is bearing an important role in future development, particularly of developing countries. This will enshrine in future fulfilment of common man's basic minimum needs, ecological soundness and self-reliance not only at the national level whether village, block and participative decision making of all levels.

The main objectives of the Council are:[55]

(i) To advise State Government in formulating science and Technology policy and programmes.
(ii) Development and transfer of appropriate technologies.
(iii) Pooling and a change of scientific knowledge.
(iv) Promotion, popularization, research, development and dissemination of Science, Technology and Environment in H.P.

The State Council for Science, Technology and Environment, H.P. located in Shimla and functioning effectively under the countrywide programme for the Department of Science and Technology, Government of India to promote Science and Technology in the States in more effective manner.

The H.P. State Council has been able to catalyze a number of Science and Technology programmes relevant to the State. The Council has also provided a number of Science and Technology inputs to the Development Departments demonstrating various technologies in the field. The Council advices the State Government on important policy issues relating to environmental conservation and development and Science and Technology interventions for the benefit of the State. The Council has a small group of Scientific working and specializing in the areas of:

(a) Science Popularising and Technology, dissemination
(b) Natural Resource Management
(c) Ecology and Environment
(d) Remote Sensing Technology, Applications
(e) Development of Voluntary Sector.

Objectives and Functions of the Council

The basic functions of the Society related to the environment conservation and development in the State are:

(i) To lay down policy and watching implementation programmes, transfer of technology, pooling and exchange of knowledge for awareness, popularization, research development and dissemination related to Science, Technology and Environment in Himachal Pradesh.

(ii) Identification of new technology, voluntary agencies, educational and R&D institutions, individuals involved in popularization of science and developing science, technology and environment related works.

(iii) Identification of new technologies for Agriculture, Industry, Power, Horticulture, Environment, Energy, etc.

(iv) All matters relating for propagation of new technologies towards environment development.

(v) Involvement of Science and Technology in the field of rural development with introducing environmental technologies in rural areas.

(vi) All matters relating to liaison with Research Institutions, National Laboratories, Universities, Department of Science and Technology and Department of Environment, Government of India.

(vii) Development of new technology towards environment protection in the State and providing consultancy services.

(viii) Providing transfer technology, assistance, act as think tank, arrange brain-storming sessions of academicians, intellectuals, administrators, researchers, field specialists for pooling knowledge in eco-system.

(ix) Promote location-specific research, demonstrate through model experiments by institutions of excellence in the State.

(x) Utilization of local capabilities and local resource on integrated basis.

(xi) Ensure application of S&T to solve real problems encountered in plan implementation through pilot projects demonstration, etc.

(xii) To initiate, support, promote and coordinate preferably by establishing network such a research, design and development projects related to environmental conservation and optimum utilization of natural resources of the State.

(xiii) To prepare assist in the preparation of Science, Technology and Environment plans of the State.

(xiv) Create specific programme-terms, task forces, coordination groups, etc. consisting of the required Science, Technology and Environment professionals and specialists.

(xv) To create Science and Technology facilities in the state towards environmental related programmes.

Orgnisational Set-up

The State Council for Science Technology and Environment, Himachal Pradesh is contributing significant role to the overall development of Himachal Pradesh. The Council has introduced a number of technologies in the State, which have benefited the common masses. The council has also been in the forefront of the campaign for creating awareness about environmental issues. This is only possible through the effective planning, programmes and projects executed by the functionaries of the council for the development of the State by introducing new ideas for using science and technological advancements.

The organizational structure of the Council can be summarily viewed from the Orgnisational Chart[56] as given below:

The administrative set-up of the Council is based on two apex bodies. The general body is headed by the Chief Minister and Minister (S&T) is the Vice-Chairman of the general body. The Finance Commissioner-cum-Secretary (S&T) is the Chairman of Executive Committee comprises of overall coordination and general supervision of the functioning of the Council. Both these apex bodies as per to the statutory provisions, are entrusted with overall responsibility and accountability for the proper running of various activities to desired end.

The overall functioning of the Council is based on its Member-Secretary along with Joint Member Secretary who are responsible for managing the business of the State Council for Science, Technology and Environment, H.P. The Scientific set-up of the Council, regarding technical activities are divided on four cells such as Remote Sensing, Science Popularisation and Dissemination, Ecology and Environment and HRD and Documentation. These cells are headed and controlled by technical experts.

Environmental Conservation Programmes

The State Council for Science, Technology and Environment, H.P. has taken number of initiatives under its activities towards environmental conservation and development in Himachal Pradesh. The Council has undertaken various programmes related to popularize the use of recycled waste products along with the research and development work on Waste Management to pilot projects.

Hospital Waste Management: An Initiative

The management of biomedical waste is the major problem in India as well as in Himachal Pradesh. Many time it has been seen that the biomedical wastes are thrown at the backyard of the hospitals. Most of time used disposable material such as syringes, needles thrown by the hospital staff is picked up by the ragpickers and are resold which further aggravates the problem. Biomedical waste is more hazardous and infectious and may pose a threat on survival of human beings along with environmental problems. Implementation of Hospital Waste Management is a challenge for the medical personnel and the municipal bodies specially in hilly areas, where the adequate disposable technology is not available. In the hilly areas methodology adopted for Waste Management largely depend upon the locality i.e. the technology has to be area specific with separate methodologies for lower, middle and altitude districts of the State.

Hospital Waste Management can be primarily dealt with following major areas of interventions:

- (i) In house segregation of the Hospital waste.
- (ii) Appropriate technology for disposal.
- (iii) Implementation of waste management and the role of different players/stake holders

The State Council is organising various training workshop on Hospital Waste Management for the safety and environmental conservation point of view in the State. The main issues of the workshops were:

- Segregation of biomedical wastes.
- Transportation of biomedical wastes.
- Training and awareness component.

Training workshops were organized on Hospital Waste Management in IGMC and Kamla Nehru Hospital. The focus of the workshop was the implementation of the Biomedical Waste Management Rules, Training for Model Systems of Hospital Waste Management, Worker and Community Safety and Technology options. The recommendations of the workshop were as follows:

- Every hospital should have dedicated autoclaves systems of variable size for destroying the laboratory media, vaccine and repeated autoclaving of reusable glass syringes and needles.
- Disposable require to be disinfected by chemical means immediately after use, right at source. These all are to be mutilated and packed in the bags as per the approved colour coding, which can be sent for deep burial or the land filling areas.
- The solid linen should be segregated and pretreated at the point of generation before mixing with other linen.
- Different bins and coloured bags of adequate size for each type of waste need to be placed at each point of generation in the hospital.
- The hospital should ensure the use of needle destroyers, which would burn the tip of the needle and cut the syringes.
- Trolleys need to be designed to carry waste from the point of generation to final disposal site in the hospital.

The other key issues with regarding to planning, a Waste Management in Hospital are related to frame detailed plan in consultation with Hospital Administration. Training and capacity building of doctors, administrators, nurses, technicians, ward boys and safai karamcharies is required. Steps such as survey, meeting of the HOD, formation of waste management committee, formal training of staff, placement of bins, monitoring of segregation, refresher courses for staff help in implementing and stabilization of system.

Conservation and Management of Wetlands

Himachal Pradesh encompasses a wide variety of natural and artificial wetlands from the sub-tropical to trans-Himalayan regions. Wetlands occupy one per cent of the total geographical area of the State. The total numbers of wetlands in the State are 92, out of which 7 are manmade and remaining 85 natural. Out of these, 3 wetlands have been identified as Wetlands of National Importance by the Ministry of Environment and Forests, GOI viz. Renuka (District Sirmour), Chandertal Lake (Spiti) and Pong Dam Wetland (District Kangra). The Ministry of Environment and Forests has been funding for the conservation and development of these National Wetlands.

The Wetland Expert Committee is working for preparation of Management Action Plan in respect of conservation and development of Wetlands in Himachal Pradesh with the assistance of State Council for Science, Technology and Environment, Himachal Pradesh. The surveys and mapping of the Wetlands has been completed and engineering structures constructions have been already developed to check the rate of siltation of wetlands in Himachal Pradesh. Further, the regular water quality of wetlands is also monitored and various plantations have been raised in these wetlands catchments areas along with the socio-economic studies of the wetlands.

The Council is also taking initiative to implement the various plans and projects to check the siltation, undertaking of works like afforestation, soil conservation and check dams to achieve the objective of environmental protection and development in the State. The council is also organising awareness camps for local communities to appraise them about the importance of conservation of wetlands eco-system.

Biodiversity Conservation and Monitoring

The State Council formulated capacity building of Community Organisations for Biodiversity, Conservation and Monitoring in Himachal Pradesh under AUSAID Project for involving local people in biodiversity assessment and monitoring. The basis of works was to establish a pilot project in biodiversity capacity building with a village community so that flora and fauna trends and consequent environmental impacts could be monitored.

The main objective of the project is to develop biodiversity mapping and monitoring methodologies for Himalayan Areas for the use of the local communities.

The National Biodiversity Strategy and Action Plan is a two year (2000-2001) project initiated by the Ministry of Environment and Forest (MOEF), Government of India and being funded by United Nations Development Programme (UNDP). It aims to formulate local, regional, state, National strategies and Action Plans for conserving biodiversity for sustainably using biological resources and achieving equity and fair benefit sharing in such use. The NBSAP was conceived by the Ministry of Environment and Forests after extensive consultations and is being executed by MOEF through a technical and policy core groups (TPCG) consisting of experts from different fields being coordinated by the Environmental Action NGO *Kalpvriksha* and its administration being handled by the Biotech Consortium India Limited (BCIL).

The Ministry of Environment and Forests has prepared a National Policy Macro level Action Strategy on biodiversity. There is need to prepare micro level action plans at State and Regional levels based on these framework.

For developing the State level plans a nodal agency like State Council for Science and Technology and Environment will act as facilitator, which will work under the guidance of a state steering committee to be appointed by the State Government with members from various government departments.

The Council has prepared certain manual including flora and fauna for diversity mapping and monitoring and identified pilot project area to involve the village level community for the environmental upgradation by way of certain projects in the State.

Keeping in view, the importance of biodiversity conservation and monitoring, the Council has undertaken provisions for the training programmes for its technical officials in India and abroad to familiar with the problem.

National Environment Awareness Campaign

The State Council for Science, Technology and Environment, H.P. has been designated as a Regional Resource Agency (RRA) since 1996 for Himachal Pradesh by the Ministry of Environment and Forests, Government of India for conducting and coordination of Environment Awareness Campaign in the State by involving NGO's, Educational Institutions and Panchayats, etc.

During the year 1998-1999, the NEAC theme was "Keep our water resource clean," State Council as an RRA coordinated the NEAC in the State by involving NGO's, Educational Institutions and Government Agencies in which 56 organisations participated. The main objective of the campaign was to get the feedback through the active interaction with experts and getting appraisal of activities carried out by the organisations. The main focus of the workshop was awareness, training and capacity building of NGOs to keep the water resources clean and regenerate traditional water resources apart from conjunctive use of technology and traditional wisdom.

The technical aspects on water resources were dealt elaborately in the workshop with the participants. Information on current Status of Water Resources and maintenance, community level environment action, Water quality, monitoring and its treatment, rainwater harvesting and Water Quality Testing were provided to the participants.

Biotechnology-based Initiatives

The State Council has taken initiatives towards biotechnology use in the State. Following are the some of initiatives launched by the State Council for Science, Technology and Environment:

- Area for Bio-Technology Interventions identified.

- Efforts made to popularise the concept of Tissue Culture for Commercialization of Horticulture and Agriculture Crops.
- Efforts being made to convert Biomass of Pine Needles and Lantana for preparation of briquettes.
- Efforts are on in collaboration with Indian Institute of Sciences, Banglore for generation of Cooking Gas from Biomass of Pine Needles and Lantana for cooking.
- Training being imparted hardening of tissue culture raised plants in green house/field conditions to progressive farmers.

Ban on Coloured Recycled Polythene Carry Bags

Plastic bags litter has become a big environment hazard in the urban areas of the State. Because of the durability and cost factor, plastic has entered into urban as well as rural areas. The increased use of plastic bags has led to mass disposal of garbage in these bags especially in the semi-urban and urban regions of Himachal Pradesh.

Himachal Pradesh is the first State in the country to have enacted an Act for dealing with Solid Waste Management and Menace of Plastic bags. The H.P. Non Biodegradable Garbage Control Act[57] was formulated by the State Council for Science, Technology and Environment, Government of H.P. enacted in 1995, to prevent throwing or disposing non-biodegradable garbage in public drains, roads and places open to public view in the State. Under Section 7(h) of the Act, prohibition was imposed on the retailers, traders and vendors for using the coloured polythene carry bags manufactured from recycled plastic, for packaging the goods traded sold by them, with effect from 1 January, 1999.

The special problems of plastic bags in this hilly State are:

(i) Availability of open slopes where municipal wastes are indiscriminately thrown.
(ii) The retention of waste on the slopes causes further problems as these wastes into the drainage system and polluted the water sources specifically of the rural areas down stream.
(iii) The polythene bags have created problems by chocking

the sewerage and drainage systems and also by virtue of the fact that polythene is non-biodegradable, thereby remaining on the slopes as such for years.

(iv) The municipal wastes are not easily collected because of the problem of access (transport and roads).

(v) Disposal of solid waste is presently being done on the slopes as large landfill sites are not available.

(vi) Recycling of used and thrown coloured polythene bags is not economically viable for the waste pickers in the hills because of the efforts it would entail and the cost of transportation.

(vii) This massive and yet scattered dumping of waste in plastic bags has led to offensive eyesores, causing increase pollution in the soil as well as the water sources.

The power have been delegated to Assistant Commissioner, Sanitary Inspectors in Shimla Municipal Corporation, Secretaries of all Nagar Panchayats, Sanitary, Inspectors in Municipal Councils, All District Food and Supplies Controller, All Inspectors (F&S) both grade I and grade II, All weights and measures Inspectors in the State.

Rain Water Harvesting

The State of Himachal Pradesh receives 1134 mm of average annual rainfall, there is a shortage of water in almost all the urban settlements of the State. The major mode of water supply in the State is through lift schemes, which are quite expensive. It is pertinent to note that only a fraction of domestic water supply is utilized for drinking purpose, and 95 per cent of water supplied to the household utilized for the purposes other than drinking and cooking viz. bathing, flushing of water closets, washing of utensils and clothes, watering of garden etc. Keeping in view the problem of scarcity of water in the urban areas of Himachal Pradesh, the Council proposed the following measures for tackling the issue of rainwater harvesting:[58]

- All buildings constructed within the urban limits of the

towns of H.P. in future will have a separate rain water collection tank as a compulsory feature. No building designs and plans will be approved if they do not include rainwater harvesting as part of essential services. The concerned local authority would finalise these details in consultation with the Department of Science and Technology, Government of Himachal Pradesh.

- All commercial institutional buildings, tourist complexes, industrial complexes, hotels, etc., existing or proposed and having plinth area more than 1000 sq. meters situated anywhere in the State will have rainwater storage facilities commensurate with the size of roof area and requirements of the place. The Department of Science and Technology, Government of H.P. would assist the concerned authority dealing with NOC in deciding the design, dimension and types of the storage tanks.
- Toilet flush systems should be connected with the rainwater collection systems. There should however be backup system for linking this with the piped water supply to meet the demand during period when the rainwater tanks are empty.
- The use of public water for watering lawns and gardens should be restricted. Instead collected rainwater should be used for this purpose.

Based on the above proposal the cabinet approved that rainwater storage will be compulsory;

(i) For all the residential buildings which come up in the urban areas of the State in future

(ii) For all the commercial/institution in future and having plinth area of more than 1000 sq. meters located anywhere in the State.

State of Environment Report

The State Council has brought out a publication titled, "State Environment Report." This report contains information and data for various facets of environment. This report comprises contributions from bureaucrats, technocrats and professionals working in different institutions. On the basis of State Environment Report a policy document on the recommendations of the expert has also been prepared. The basic objectives of this report are:[59]

- To identify issues which need attention of planners and policy-makers for sectoral development.
- To redefine indicative and operational roles for the Government in the environment problem solving trend modifying and opportunity seeking.
- To define policy frames and implementation mechanism.
- Environmental database for policy formulation.
- To identify the role of people in environment conservation, protection and rehabilitation.

This report comprises of contributions of different professionals and experts working in different sectors. The Report will definitely to be realized as citizen voices and will reflect the views of experts, specialists, thinkers towards environmental conservation and development plans, policies, programmes and projects.

Solar Passive Technology

Himachal Pradesh is the first State in the country to introduce Solar Passive Building Technology in the design and construction of Government and Semi-Government buildings on large scale.

The State Council for Science, Technology and Environment, H.P. formulated the Solar House Action Plan for Himachal Pradesh in May 1994,[60] which is being supported by Ministry of Non-Conventional Sources, Government of India . The Council is co-ordinating the Passive Solar Building Programme in Himachal Pradesh in collaboration with HPPWD and H.P. Housing Board.

Solar Passive Building Technology utilized the orientation of building and the availability of solar energy as the site for heating of buildings resulting in saving of large amounts of fossil fuels and electricity required for space heating in winter.

Himachal Pradesh Government has taken an important policy

decision for the implementations of Solar Passive Building Technology in the State on August 2000, which states:

- Solar Passive design for the implementation of Solar Passive House Action Plan for Himachal Pradesh.
- All the departments including corporations, boards, universities, H.P. Housing Board, HPPWD and H.P. Nagar Vicks Pradhikaran to have incorporate features of Solar passive technology in their designs at places about 2000 meter (msl.).

Keeping in view the importance of this technology in Himachal Pradesh to save the environment degradation by utilizing Solar Passive Heating System Technology, the State Council for Science, Technology and Environment, H.P. is the nodal Agency for this plan for which the funds are provided by the Ministry of Non-Conventional Energy Sources, Government of India and Government of Himachal Pradesh. The council has set up a Technical Project Management Cell for the implementation of this plan, which is already co-ordinating with architectural and engineering wings of State Housing Agencies. This cell has scientific, architectural and engineering staff and panel of solar experts. A number of training workshops in Solar Passive Housing Technology has been organized by the State Council is providing the Solar Passive Design of 25 buildings in government/ semi-government sectors.

These buildings have been designed as per Solar Passive buildings out of which, nineteen buildings namely State Bank of Patiala, H.P. Cooperative Bank Building, HIMURJA Building, MLA Hostel (4 Blocks), Minister's House (6 blocks), Judge's House (5 Blocks) at Shimla, 300 bed Government Hospital Khaneri, Rampur and Tabo Monastry Sarai (Spiti) have already been constructed.

Further, 15 Solar Passive Primary Schools at Hul, Rangrik, Sagham, Morang in Spiti, Maghara, Kayari, Bhavnoli, Radhar, Jagoti Nala, Limbra, Pujarli, Thana, Saroli and Higeri (District Shimla) have been constructed for which design was provided by the Council to District Administration and Rural Development Department.

Council has provided new design of Teacher's Hostel, which

has a number of solar passive features like proper orientation, sun spaces, cavity walls, root insulation. Two Solar Passive designed teachers hostels at Sangam and Tabo (Spiti) have been constructed and seven are under construction in Spiti and District Shimla.

In rural and tribal areas of the State, the Council has retrofitted 12 traditional houses with low cost thermos phoning air heating panels, Sunspace and Trombe wall systems in Spiti, Sangla Valley (Kinnaur and Sachuin village, Bharmour (Distt. Chamba).

Keeping in view the above factors in consistorian, it has been observed that Passive Solar Building Technology is an environmentally sound and economically viable technology. The State Council for Science, Technology and Environment, H.P. is providing such environment-friendly technology in the State with the assistance of the Ministry of Non-Conventional Energy Sources, for efficient functional planning, energy efficiency and protection of eco-system in the State.

Remote Sensing Technology: Idea and Action

Remote Sensing Technology has opened up new vistas for natural resources inventory and minority with the extension of the capability to took beyond the visible part of the electro-magnetic spectrum. Humankind now has access to information hitherto unknown to him. Synoptic perspective and repetitive coverage available from orbital satellites has add new dimensions in monitoring the dynamic aspects of the Geo-environment. The successful launch of IRS series of satellites and availability of high resolution stereoscopic images at 5.6 m resolution will further enhance the application potential. Remote sensing cell of the State Council for Science, Technology and Environment is making earnest efforts to use the modern technology of Remote Sensing in assessing and making inventory of the natural resources of the State. Assessment of ground water, snow and glaciers and micro hydel potential of the State is an ongoing activity of the Remote Sensing Cell.[61]

To harness the potential of this modern tool, Himachal Pradesh Remote Sensing Cell was established as a wing of the State Council for Science, Technology and Environment in the year 1989 to achieve the following objectives:[62]

(1) To create centralized facilities and infrastructure by obtaining satellite data, interpretation aids and ancillary collateral data for the use of all potential users.
(2) To create an effective information centre based on aerospace data encompassing different themes for the use of geographical information system and related software for various planning programmes.
(3) To provide specialized assistance to various user agencies and institutes in the field of their interests based on Remote Sensing inputs.
(4) To impart training and education in the use of cost-effective space technology in the field of national resources management.

The State Council with the help of its Scientists having expertise in different fields and have developed the capability to undertake the various activities such as: Water Resources Surveys; Land-use Surveys, Natural Hazard Assessment, Urban and Regional Planning; Environment Impact Assessment, Wetland Management Planning; Snow Cover Assessment, Geotechnical Surveys; Natural Resource Mapping; Eco-Tourism Planning; Training and Support Services and Consultancy Services within the State to achieve the environment conservatory of Environment and Forests. Harnessing of space technology for natural resource inventory and accelerating the process of education and training is high on the agenda of the concern and development in Himachal Pradesh.

The various facilities provided by the State Council in the area of Remote Sensing have been created in the State with the use of satellite data. The various facilities in Remote Sensing based studies have been provided and been completed.

- Hydrogeomorphological mapping of the entire State on Scale.
- Land-use mapping of the entire State on Scale.
- Lineament mapping of the entire state.
- Delineation and generation of digital data of the wasteland in 9 districts of the State.
- Wetland inventory of the entire State prepared and digital

database made available to fisheries department.

- Integrated evaluation of natural resources of Chamba district on scale generation of digital database for planning.
- Geographical information facility has been established in the State and training to user departments provided.
- Consultancy services were also provided to Rail India Technical Economic Services, Delhi in carrying out geotechnical feasibility of proposed tunnel across Rohtang ridge.
- Studies were also carried out for assessing the status of limestone mining in Sirmour and slate mining in Kangra districts.
- Assessment of tea plantation in Kangra district was also carried out.
- Glacier lands now cover mapping for the entire Satluj and Beas basins completed.
- Digital database and Atlas prepared at the scale has been handed over to HPSEB and HIMURJA. Data has been utilized for identifying locations for micro hydel projects.

Water Management

The State Council of Science, Technology and Environment has undertaken the various activities related to water resources management in the State for tapping ground water resources and construction of rainwater harvesting structure and conservation of water bodies.

For scientific sources finding the Remote and Sensing Cell has carried out Remote Sensing Survey to identify potential pockets where ground water can be tapped with the help of Remote Sensing Surveys and ground-based hydro geological surveys. One of the most outstanding contribution of the State Council of Science, Technology and Environment, H.P. has been the popularization of India Mark II and III hand pumps for extracting ground water from the deeper horizons. The Council has also organized community training and awareness programmes to undertake repair and maintenance work of hand pumps by the villagers themselves.

The another area in which State Council is providing assistance is Hydro-geomorphological Mapping and Development of

Ground Water in H.P. funded by Department of Space, GOI for development of water in the State. Table 4.1 provides a detail of hand pump facility in the State more than 10,000 villages have been covered:

TABLE 4.1: Number of Hand Pumps Installed in Collaboration with UNICEF and I&PH in Himachal Pradesh

Year	UNICEF	I&PH
1990-91	31	–
1991-92	69	323
1992-93	–	789
1993-94	–	1496
1994-95	–	1000
1995-96	–	1001
1996-97	–	809
1997-98	–	712
1998-99	–	792
1999-2000	–	1019
2000-2001	–	900
Total	100	8846
Grand Total		8946

Source: Department of I &PH, Government of Himachal Pradesh.

Summing up

The Council for Science, Technology and Environment, H.P. has contributed significantly to the overall development of Himachal Pradesh and particularly in Environment protection and conservation. The Council has been also in the forefront of the campaign for creating awareness about environmental issues.

On the initiative of the H.P. Government, the Council has taken a number of important policy decisions to maintain overall development of the society with the help of science and technological advancements for the benefits of the rural masses of Himachal Pradesh.

The Council has introduced a number of technologies like

water management rough hand pumps, rooftop rainwater harvesting, and solar passive housing technology, remote sensing and solid waste management in environmental issues. Brief account of the activities of the council encompasses the broad spectrum of interventions the Council has made over the last one decade. The Council is a small group of scientific and technical personnel who have successfully focused the public attention, the attention of the Government policy-makers and planners on issues of vital importance for improving the life style of common man; a man in the village. The mandate given to the State Council can broadly be stated as to popularize and utilize science and technology for the optimum development of natural resources of the State. Identification of technologies, identification of problems, popularizing the concept and coordinating the efforts with concerned departments and then facilitating the implementation of the idea on ground are some of the important functions of the Council.

Tapping the Solar Energy for comforting the life of people living in the higher altitude is another area where the Council has made considerable efforts. Further, creating awareness amongst the public on issues of environmental concern is another area, which has engaged the attention of the Council. Important issues like controlling the nuisance of polythene have been successfully brought in the forefront, on which the Government has initiated policy and legislative measures. Similarly, rooftop rainwater harvesting has been made mandatory in the urban areas to conserve water and recharge ground water table. The council is also effectively acting as state mode for the departments like Department of Space, Ministry of Non-Conventional Energy, Ministry of Science, Technology and Ministry of Environment and Forests. Harnessing of space technology for natural resource inventory and accelerating the process of education and training is high on the agenda of the Council.

5

Sustainable Development and Environment

Degradation of the environment because of improper channelization of resources and rapid expansion of the population create a state of instability, which destroys the life-supporting system of the earth and ensure ultimate economic collapse. A move towards sustainable development aims at meeting the needs of the world's present population without so eroding its natural resources that future generations are enable to satisfy theirs.

Sustainable development is the development that lasts. It means,[63] "meeting the needs of the present without compromising the ability of future generations to meet their own needs". Through sustainable development our environment can be protected, our economy can be grow and our society can be well off all simultaneously. Sustainability comprises three major human activities: production, distribution and consumption. These activities in turn depend on the costs involved, benefits derived and means through which they could be achieved. Further, sustainability has various dimensions—quantitative and qualitative, short-term and long-term. In the context of sustainable natural resource-use, inter-generational equity of optimization is also to be considered seriously. Clearly sustainable development must benefit both current and future generation. Sustainability requires alleviation of poverty, a decline in fertility, the substitution of human capital for natural resources, effective demand for environmental quality, and a responsive supply. These changes cannot take place on a sustainable basis without growth.

Sustainable development is also defined with reference to three parameters.[64] First, it concerns protecting environment and avoiding depletion of non-renewable resources. It requires shifting from reliance on one resource to another. Second, it refers to equity i.e. equal access to resources. Finally the concept of sustainable development must concerns integrational distribution of resources.

Keeping in view the importance of sustainable development, energy is major requirement for the economic, agricultural and industrial growth of any country or society. Hence there is an ever-increasing demand for energy in it's various forms. Energy plays pivotal and important role in the economic development. The growth in energy consumption is more rapid in developing countries as compare to developed countries. As they seek to industrialize, raise standard of living and accommodate population growth, energy requirements of the developing countries are relatively higher.

The seriousness of rural energy crises and its complex nature was recognize by the Planning Commission and National Rural Energy Planning exercise was started in the year 1981 for developing approach for planning and implementation of Integrated Rural Energy Planning Programme (IREP).

In Himachal Pradesh, this exercise was started in the terminal year of Sixth Plan. Energy Surveys were carried out to formulate an action plan so as to implement these programmes. The programmes were initially started on pilot basis in two blocks i.e. Theog (Shimla) and Spiti (Lahaul & Spiti) of the state and latter extended to 45 blocks. While formulating the action plan of implementing Integrated Rural Energy Planning Programme in the State, efforts were made to supplement rural energy needs by exploiting the non-conventional energy sources.

HIMURJA: An Introduction

In order to give more thrust to Integrated Rural Energy Planning Programme (IREP) and to institutationalise the various programmes of non-conventional energy sources, which are aptly suited for decentralized applications in the state. HIMURJA (H.P. Energy Development Agency) was established in February, 1989 by H.P. Government under the Chairmanship of Hon'ble Chief

Minister to promote and popularize renewable and appropriate energy systems at affordable prices, among the public and also to encourage R&D efforts in the renewal energy sector. Renewal energy sources are sustainable, providing clean energy. The decentralized renewal system has now been recognized world over as an alternative to meet the growing needs.

HIMURJA is committed to evolve an optimal energy plan for the state particularly in the rural sector, so that the conventional energy consumption is reduced, environmental and ecological balances are maintained, and quality life is improved.

Administrative Setup

Headquarters Office being at the apex generally concerns itself with the Chief Executive Officer and Director is responsible for direction, control of policy and appraisal of performance, overall health of the Agency, forward planning and co-ordination. The apex level control overall at the top-level functions, such as capital investment decisions, management innovations, long-range planning, organizational structuring, financial and personal decisions, laying down management of objectives, executive development, advisory services overall co-ordination and general supervision of various complexes i.e. the block offices of the Agency. The organizational Administrative structure of the agency summarily given below.

The Chief Executive Officer along with the Director of the Agency occupies the top of hierarchical ladder. Next in the hierarchy, of the headquarter comes Joint Director, who is responsible for the proper functioning, co-ordinating and implementing the various policies and programmes of the Agency. Executive Engineers (Civil & Electrical) are immediately next to the Joint Director and are responsible for overall technical activities of the Agency. They are also entrusted with overall control and supervision of various technical works operated at block offices in the State. Further, for the proper functioning the headquarter's office is assisted by an Account Officer, Superintendent, Junior Engineers, Investigator, computer operator and other office assistance staff. There is a provision for staff deployed from HPSEB under Micro Hydel,

Wind Energy Programme, having two Assistant Engineers and two Junior Engineers.

At the field level i.e. the block offices of the Agency are headed by the Project Officer. He is assisted with Junior Engineer for the functioning of the agency along with office staff.

Executive Committee

In order to supervise and control the Agency's activities, both financial and administrative, an Executive Committee has been constituted with following members:

1.	Secretary (ST&E) Government of HP	Chairman
2.	Secretary (Finance) H.P. Government or his authorized representative	Member
3.	Secretary (Forests) H.P. Government or his authorized representative	Member
4.	Secretary (MPP and Power) H.P. Government or his authorized representative	Member
5.	Director Agriculture, Himachal Pradesh	Member
6.	Director, RDD, Himachal Pradesh	Member
7.	Advisor (Planning) Himachal Pradesh	Member
8.	Chief Executive Officer, HIMURJA	Member-Secretary

The success of any complex organisation depends upon the teamwork of a devoted, competent and efficient Executive Committee. Responsibility for proper running of an agency rests with its Executive Committee. A proper composition of Executive Committee is very important for the success of any organisation for its assigned purposes.

The Executive Committee of the Energy Development Agency is responsible for managing the business. The committee determines broad policies and exercises such control as will satisfy it that these policies are being carried out. It approves the capital expenditure, sets out Agency's objectives and strategies assigns responsibilities and authorities to the Chief Executive Officer and Director, and makes all senior appointments.

The Executive Committee as a subsidiary legislature authority of the Agency derives its various powers under the constitutional framework of the Agency, for overall working and achievements.

With regard to major financial matters of the Agency, the Executive Committee has the authority to take various decisions and to frame policy on financial matters. Thus the Executive Committee's direct responsibilities are:

(a) to set overall policy objective for the Agency;
(b) to review and approve strategic plans for the achievement of these objectives;
(c) to decide on entry into new fields of Agency's activities;
(d) to approve development and annual operating plans;
(e) to approve or delegate the authorization of all capital expenditure; and
(f) to take decision on all matters delegated by the Agency.

Integrated Rural Energy Planning Programme

Solar Energy utilisation forms an important part of the new and renewal sources of energy. HIMURJA has made concerted efforts to popularize renewal energy through the Integrated Rural Energy Planning Programme (IREP), which has been taken up as full-fledged programme in 45 blocks in Himachal Pradesh with the financial support of Ministry of Non-Conventional Energy Sources (MNES), Government of India. Efforts are also being made to propagate fuel-efficient devices like Solar cookers, solar water heating systems, solar dryers, improved chullahas, improved water mills, and photovoltaic lights (for IRDP families, etc.).

Programmes of HIMURJA

HIMURJA has been constituted to promote and popularize renewal and provide appropriate energy system at affordable prices, among the larger public through implementation of Integrated Rural Energy Planning Programme in various blocks of the Pradesh and also encourage R&D efforts in the renewal energy sector.

The biogas, improved chullah, Solar thermal and Solar PV

Programme received initial thrust with the launching of IRDP in the selected districts, Micro level integrated energy planning is also being encouraged for holistic development of selected IREP blocks. Till now the different schemes have been promoted with the help of Central/State subsidies and incentives after determining their cost benefits.

In order to exploit small Hydro Power Generation in the cost-effective manner with private sector participation, the State Government has made several administrative arrangements. The task of providing Single Window Services in terms of inviting, processing application of private investors, clearances and signing of implementation Agreement/Power Purchase Agreements has been entrusted to HIMURJA under the administrative control MPP and Power Department.

The activities of HIMURJA can be categorized into three groups:

(a) Solar Energy Utilisation through Solar Thermal and Photovoltaic Roots
(b) Energy Conservation
(c) Small Hydro Programme

(a) *Solar Energy Utilisation*

Solar Energy is an exhaustible source of renewal energy and can be utilized through two principle routes:

(a) Solar Thermal;
(b) Solar Photovoltaic

Solar Thermal

Apart from encouraging the fuel-efficient and alternative sources of energy for selecting IREP blocks, the programme pertaining to harnessing solar energy, mini micro hydel project and wind energy are other areas which was also taken up by HIMURJA. Various devices adopted through solar thermal route and photovoltaic route are being encouraged. Keeping in view the realistic view of existing possibilities in proven technologies devices such as Solar Water Heating System, Solar Cooker and PV Lights, etc. is being provided subsidized.

The different temperature ranges, which can be generated by various solar thermal devices, include:

(i) Low-grade thermal energy, which covers the temperature range below 100°C, the most common applications of which are water heating, air heating, drying, etc.
(ii) Medium grade thermal energy which covers the temperature range from 100°C to 300°C whose applications include cooking, industrial process heat, low pressure, steam generation, refrigeration, water pumping, etc.,
(iii) High grade thermal energy, which covers temperatures above 300°C, and has the main application of power generation and processing of materials.

HIMURJA has made efforts to popularize solar thermal devices like Solar Cooker, water heating systems, solar dryers, etc. The progress made up to February 2001 is as follows:

- 27,384 Solar Cookers have been distributed in the State upto February, 2001.
- 2746 Solar Water Heating Systems of different capacities with a total capacity of 4,63,600 LPD (liter per day) have been installed/booked in different parts of the State.
- The Government of H.P. has taken a decision to make the installation of Solar Water Heating Systems mandatory in all Government Buildings/Institutions, etc. In the first phase Solar Water Heating System of 10,000 LPD S.W.H.S. in Zonal Hospital at Dharamshala, 2000 LPD S.W.H.S. in Raj Bhavan at Shimla, 2000 LPD S.W.H.S. at H.P. Secretariat, 2000 LPD S.W.H.S. at HIMURJA building have already been installed. The work of installation of 20,000 LPD of S.W.H.S. in Indira Gandhi Medical College, Shimla and 10,000 LPD at Zonal Hospital, Khaneri, Rampur and Himachal Bhawan, Chandigarh (12000 LPD) has also been completed.

Solar Photovoltaic Programmes

Though hundred percent electrification has been achieved in Himachal Pradesh, yet there are number of hamlets and small pockets of houses, which are still unelectrified. Some of these houses are so remotely located that the people living there can not hope for electrification by conventional means since it is not possible to lay the transmission/distribution lines for covering these areas as it is a very costly proposition. The only alternative for electrification of such a multitude of hamlets/pockets of houses is by providing solar photovoltaic systems for decentralized application.

After the successful experiences of electrifying the houses in Kunnu and Charang, Shalkhar villages in Kinnaur district, HIMURJA has identified some other remote locations in H.P. for this purpose.

The number of 1183 Solar P.V. Street Lights, 9939 Domestic P.V. Lights and 21679 Solar P.V. Lanterns have been distributed at subsidized rates in different IREP Blocks in the Pradesh upto March 2001.

(b) *Energy Conservation Programme*

In order to conserve energy, HIMURJA been providing energy efficient devices like Pressure Cookers, Nutan Stoves and Nutan Jyoti, etc. to identified IRDP families in the selected IREP blocks. So far 103847 pressure cookers, 26881 Nutan Jyoti and 41824 Nutan Stoves have been provided to IRDP families on subsidized rate. The various schemes of the Agency are provided below:

- A number of 13459 improved chullahs were distributed in different selected block upto March 2001.
- The improved high altitude portable Chullahs for cooking and space heating purpose, has been developed with increased thermal efficiency of 45 per cent and is being popularized in cold regions and tribal areas (more than 6000 ft) 10997. Such chullahs have been distributed on subsidy in the tribal areas upto March, 2001.

- A number of 1073 improved wheels (Gharats) with improved efficiency have also been installed in different parts of the State.

(c) *Micro Hydel Programme in Himachal Pradesh*

The State of Himachal Pradesh has a vast hydro-electric potential of about 20,000 MW out of which about 4400 MW has been harnessed so far. In addition to this, there is an estimated potential of approximately 750 MW in the Micro/Small Hydro Power (SHP) sector (i.e. less than 3 MW. Out of this a potential of approximately 645 MW at 431 sites with capacities ranging from 100 KW to 3 MW has so far been identified.

In order to provide focused and undivided attention to SHP sector, the subject was transferred from HPSEB to HIMURJA by a decision of Cabinet, notified on 21st, 22nd November 1994. With this decision of the cabinet, the arrangement of providing single window services in terms of inviting, processing the applications of Private Investors, clearance and signing of Memorandum of Understanding (MOU) was entrusted to the Science and Technology Department (subsequently the Administrative Control of HIMURJA was transferred to MPP and Power Department) and since then the institutional mechanism of HIMURJA has been utilized for this purpose.

The projects identified for private sector participation were based on preliminary investigation and remote sensing data. Therefore, it was decided to adopt MOU route for preparation of detailed project report after detailed survey and investigation. The DPRs are to be based on minimum two loan season discharge data (December to March). After the scrutiny of the DPR, the Techno-Economic Clearance (TE) is accorded by HPSEB. Thereafter the Implementation Agreement with H.P. Government and Power Purchase Agreement with HPSEB is signed by the Private Investor. The physical work for executing the project is to be taken in hand by the developers only after obtaining the statutory clearances/ NOCs and acquisition of land.

As per the private sector participation in the first phase of the private sector, the total estimated capacity of the projects ranges between 71.42 M.W. The total number of projects advertised during the first phase was 137, out of total number for 64 projects MOUs were signed.

In the second stage, total of 319 sites including 53 sites, which remained un-allotted in the first stage, with an aggregate potential of 474.95 MW were advertised for private sector participation during September, 1998.

In the third phase, total number of projects advertised were 261 for the total capacity of the project 382 MW. The total aggregate capacity of the projects was 171.77 MW allotted. The total number of projects for which MOUs signed during this phase was 66 along with aggregate capacity of the projects 101 MW.

In the final, implementation agreements/power purchase agreement have been signed by 15 companies for 23 projects. The total estimated capacity of projects for which agreements signed is 47.75 MW with total estimated cost of projects is 288 crore.

Participation of Co-operative Societies in Power Generation

In order to involve the Cooperative Societies in the establishment, operation and maintenance of micro hydel generation stations, the State Government proposed an amendment in Section-2 (4-A) of the Electricity (Supply) Act, 1948, which earlier allowed only the Companies, registered under the Company Act, 1956, to do this business. The Electricity (Supply) H.P. Second Amendment Bill, 1999 on the subject has been approved by Government of India. The amendment will enable the Cooperative Societies and Societies in the State to take up such projects.

Mini/Micro Projects being Implcmented Under UNDP-GEF Hilly

Hydro Programme

The UNDP-GEF proposal is a collaborative venture of the World Bank UNDP and over 90 National Governments, which aim to achieve reduction in global warming, protection of bio-diversity in the Himalayan and Sub-Himalayan regions and creating enhanced job opportunities.

The UNDP-GEF India Hilly Hydro Project is the first project from India to be included in the GEF (Global Environment Facility) portfolio. The following projects are under execution under UNDP-GEF Hilly Hydro Programme in H.P.

Project	Capacity (KW)	Developer	Project (Cost)
1. Lingti	400	HIMURJA	714.00
2. Kothi	200	HIMURJA	152.00
3. Juthed	100	HIMURJA	90.00
4. Purthi	100	HIMURJA	211.00
5. Sural	100	HIMURJA	211.00
6. Solang	1000	M/s A Power Himalayas Ltd., Paonta Sahib (HP)	649.60
7. Titang	800	M/s Sai Engineering Foundation, New Shimla	469.00
8. Saket	800	M/s I. Power, Ltd., New Delhi	486.00

Source: Based on the Administrative Report of the Agency.

Installation of Portable Micro Hydel Generator Sets

HIMURJA had been allocated 15 Nos. Portable Hydel Generating Sets (10 Nos. 15 Kilo Watt Capacity and 5 Nos. 10 Kilo Watt Capacity), by Ministry of Non-Conventional Energy Sources, Government of India, free of cost for installation in remote areas, out of total target of 50 Nos. Portable Generator Sets for the whole country.

12 Nos. Sets with total capacity of 155 KW have been installed in unelectrified Saichu Valley (Pangi Area) at four different locations viz. Hillour, Sahali, Saichu and Hillu Twan. These 12 Nos. generating sets with total capacity 155 KW have been commissioned and running successfully. Two Nos. of 15 KW sets have been installed in Dodra Kawar area. One Generating Set of 15 KW has been installed at Sarahan (Rampur Bushehar) as a demonstration unit.

It is proposed to charge a uniform tariff of Rs.20 per household per month (for two light points) in Pangi and Dodra Kawar areas on the pattern of NEDA (Non-Conventional Energy Development Agency, U.P.) who are charging @ Rs.32 per household.

Rehabilitation and Augmentation of Gharola (District Chamba) Micro Hydel Project (2 × 50 KW)

The work on rehabilitation of Gharola Micro Hydel Project 50 KW and its upgradation to 100 KW was entrusted to HIMURJA as per the decision of Tribal Advisory Committee Meeting held on 2nd May, 1997. The project with total estimated cost of Rs.70.00 lakh, is targeted for completion by the end of June 2001.

Hydrams Popularisation

Hydro Power at the micro level can also be utilized in a cost effective manner in the form of mechanical power through Hydraulic Ram (Hydrams). A Hydraulic-Ram (Hydrams) is an impulse pump working on the principal of water hammer. Major feature of a hydraulic ram are non-requirement of an external source of energy, low maintenance and operation costs and the requirement of some minimal head at the water source. The hydrams assume special importance in hilly areas. HIMURJA had installed 111 hydrams in different location of the State.

Ministry of Rural Development, Government of India has sanctioned two projects to install 200 Hydrams in next 4 years, in Shimla and Kullu Districts under the technology demonstration and extension scheme and 500 Hydrams under the project for Infrastructural Development in HP under SGSY special project component respectively). HIMURJA is facilitating Rural Development Department in the installation of Hydrams under these schemes in terms of procurement of machines and providing training to the potential beneficiaries for operation and maintenance.

Energy Efficient Devices: An Analysis

In Himachal Pradesh, there is a plenty of sun shine and solar energy i.e. one of the most important alternative to meet cooking and heating energy needs. Solar energy is playing a significant role in rural development especially remote areas whose fuelwood is score. Due to cold climate, hot water in Himachal Pradesh is almost a necessity for bathing, washing and other miscellaneous needs. Lot of fuelwood is used to heat water.

(i) *Solar Water Heating*

For the water heating in the State, the pressure is generally on the forests. The solar energy system saves the energy in various forms along with cost such as:

(a) Fuelwood: 2138 kg. saves Rs.2780.
(b) Kerosene Oil: 374 literes saves Rs.935.
(c) Electricity: 2230 unit saves Rs.970.

This clearly indicates that a 100 litre per day capacity solar heater is capable of saving about 2138 kg of fuelwood or 2230 KWH of electrical energy. The thermo system water heaters are becoming popular in Himachal Pradesh and thus saving the requirement of fuelwood and electricity in particular. There are 168 Solar Water Heating Systems of 54,800 liter per day of different capacity has been installed in different parts of the State. This provides an idea and action of the use of non-conventional energy system in hilly areas like Himachal Pradesh. Further, keeping in view the importance of solar energy, the government of Himachal Pradesh has taken a decision to make the installation of Solar Water Heating Systems in all the Government buildings, institutions, etc. as mandatory.

(ii) *Nutan Stoves*

Nutan stoves are another device to save energy in the State. Fuel-efficient stoves are supplied to IRDP families in the selected IREP Blocks in the State at 50 per cent cost. These stoves are saving fuel ranging between 14 per cent to 25 per cent. This is another important concept of saving fuelwood in the areas where the scarcity of forest is prevailing in the State. HIMURJA has already distributed quite number of Nutan Stoves in Himachal Pradesh to achieve the objective in broader sense.

(iii) *Improved Chullahs*

The Organisation constituted to implement NPIC to reduce the strain on the jungles and to popularize these smokeless devices for the betterment of rural household. These devices have much more efficiency ranging between 25 per cent to 35 per cent whereas the traditional chullahs have only 10 per cent working performance. Smokeless chullas have been distributed in selected IREP Blocks of the state by the Agency.

(iv) *Improved Water Wheels*

The extension cell of Government Polytechnic, Sundernagar has designed and fabricated a cast-iron turbine wheel to replace existing wooden turbine in the traditional gharats and the introduction of these wheels in gharats and modification in water conducting system have given very encouraging results in improving efficiency of gharats.

(v) *Hydrams*

Hydrams could be the most cost-effective methodology for providing minor irrigation schemes, which require high capital and O&M costs. Hydrams is a low cost appropriate technology with very low recurring costs. Popularising of this technology is also to revive the old and traditional system of beneficiaries managed irrigation system. HIMURJA is popularizing this technology in the State to achieve the efficiency and effectiveness in Hydrams.

Wind Energy

The scope for exploitation of Wind Energy in the State for power generation and other mechanical uses like lighting of ground water is being explored. The modalities to boost this programme are being worked out in consultation with MNES. A case has been taken up with MNES for the installation of Monitoring Stations at 15 places in the state to study the wind energy potential.

Table 5.1 indicates an idea of financial incentives provided by the State and Central Government regarding the various energy efficient devices in the State during the year 1998-99.

TABLE 5.1: Energy Efficient Devices in the State

Item	State Govt.	Central Govt.
1. Smokeless Chullah	Nil	Rs.40 per Chullah (with Chimney)
2. High Altitude Chullah	Nil	Rs.250 per Chullah (maximum) limited to 50% of the cost
3. Portable Chullah	Nil	Rs.75 per month
4. Energy Efficient	50% of the cost or Rs.50 whichever is less (only to identified IRDP families of IREP Blocks only)	Nil
5. Solar Cookers	Rs.200	Nil
6. Solar Water Heating Systems (I) 100 LPD	Rs.3000	Nil
7. Improved Water	50% of the cost or Rs.300 whichever is less	Nil
8. Solar Lantern	Available at Rs.1500 to SC/ST beneficiaries and Rs.2000 to others. Difference of cost is being met from State Plan	Rs.1500
9. Solar P.V. Domestic Lights	PV Domestic Light is available at Rs.3500 for the beneficiaries living in remote areas	Rs.6000 or 50% of the ex-work cost on the system
10. Nutan Jyoti Kerosene Lantern	50% of the unit cost to IRDP families of IREP Blocks	Nil

Physical Targets and Achievements

The Government of Himachal Pradesh has made certain provisions to achieve targets in the field of new and renewable resources. With the growth in the economy, the demand for energy increases tremendously due to rapid industrialization, better standard of living and increased infrastructure network. Table 5.2 gives an idea of the physical targets and achievement during the year 1998-99 achieved by the Government of Himachal Pradesh through its agency i.e. HIMURJA:

TABLE 5.2: Physical Target and Achievements

Item	Targets (1998-99)	Physical Ach. (Provisional)	Commutative (since inception	Achievements
I. Solar Thermal				
1. Solar Cooker	1000	650	26181	
2. Solar Drier	40	38	313	
3. Solar Water Heating Systems				Booked/Installed
(i) 100 LPD	100	92	2067	• Order placed for 8000 LPD (2000×4) system for Himachal Bhawan, Delhi
(ii) 200 LPD	10	8	102	
(iii) 500 LPD	50	52	280	
(iv) 1000LPD	10	14	44	
(v) 2000 LPD	-	2*	7*	• Order for the 12000 LPD for Himachal Bhawan, Chandigarh
II. Photovoltaic Systems				
1. P.V. Domestic Light	10000	1565	5958	
2. P.V. Street Light	200	62**	635	**200 systems are under installation
3. P.V. Lantern	4000	3254	16275	
III. Energy Efficient Devices				
1. Nutan Stoves (only for IRDP families)	4000	4568	39378	

(*Contd.*)

Item	Targets (1998-99)	Physical Ach. (Provisional)	Commutative (since inception	Achievements
2. Impoved Chullas/ High Alt. Chullahs	6000	7080	130143	
3. Nutan Jyoti	4000	3942	24258	
IV. MPP Project				
1. Hydrams	50	50*	71	*(Fabrication completed. 50 Nos. Hydrams supplied at sites and are under installation after testing.)
2. Imp. Water Wheel	150	150	871	
3. Portable Generator sets	2	2*	13	*(Installed but commissioning to be tested.)
4. Nos. of MHP under UNDP-GEF and rehabilitation of Gharola Project	4 Partially for civil works as per detail given below	*Details given below		
(i) Lingti (400 KW) (Civil Work)		50%	60%	
(ii) Juther (100 KW) (Civil Work)		10%	10%	
(iii) Kothi (200 KW) (Civil Work)		10%	10%	
(iv) Gharola (2 × 50 KW) Civil Work)		60%	60%	

Source: HIMURJA.

Summing Up

HIMURJA is no doubt committed to evolve an optional energy plan for the State particularly in the rural sector, so that the conventional energy is reduced, environmental and ecological balances are maintained. Today, HIMURJA is playing a pivotal role in the State in the environmental conservation and development by launching the Integrated Rural Energy Planning Programme (IREP) of non-conventional energy sources, which are suited for the state in maintaining the ecological balance. The decentralized renewal energy systems have now been recognized world over as an alternative to meet the growing needs and maintaining the ecological balance.

With the growth in population and urbanisation the energy requirements also increased in the urban as well as the rural sector, which leads to crisis to the forests and towards conventional energy. The Government of Himachal Pradesh knowing the importance of sustainable development carried out an action plan to save the forest property from the local people regarding their local needs, launched HIMURJA (An Energy Development Agency) to promote and popularize renewal energy sources in the State. This Agency is committed to achieve the objectives so that the conventional energy consumption is reduced and quality life is improved.

HIMURJA has made efforts to popularize solar thermal devices by way of distributing in the State, which seems a healthy sign of progress to achieve the desired goal. The another sector where this Agency is working hard is micro hydel programme in the State. The various projects have been signed to generate the electricity at local level with local requirements. These micro hydel projects are useful in maintaining the ecological balance in the State. This is very important for hilly state like Himachal Pradesh where big hydel projects are not suited both in safety and environmental conservation point of view. Thus, HIMURJA is playing an important role to conserve the natural resources of energy for the betterment of the human community in the State.

6

Conclusions and Policy Implications

Healthy environment is the most essential pre-requisite of human life. The problem of environment pollution has in recent times engaged the attention of most developed countries and international agencies.

There is no deny the fact that this fact has duly been recognized by the society as well as the administration that the existence of the human race depends on the existence of balanced ecological system. Government and Forest departments all over the country are also showing awareness about the ecological balance, for which forests play the most significant role.

Himachal is slightly happily placed when the figures with regard to the forest area in ratio to the total area of the State is compared to the corresponding national figures. Similarly, per capita forest area in Himachal Pradesh is more than four times that of national coverage. But Himachal Pradesh has greater constraints to face greater responsibilities to shoulder. Being hilly and snow-bound State, one-third of its area is perennially snow-covered, and thus unsuitable for the growth of any vegetation. Thus, Himachal Pradesh cannot increase its forest area as per the State Forest Policy. Further, the temperature climate of most parts of the State makes quick afforestation difficult. Only some lower valleys are suitable for fast growing vide-leaf verities of trees. But these valleys have tremendous pressure of population, roads, agriculture needs, industrialization and urbanization making it almost impossible to undertake some big scale afforestation.

Higher reaches of the State are criss-crossed with rivers, rivulets,

Nullahas, streams, ravines and valleys. Soil erosion in such terrain is a big problem. Road-building activity takes its own toll in eforestation, denuding the hills and landslides and soil erosion. Himachal shoulders have a very heavy responsibility of maintaining big irrigation and hydro-electric dams, which besides submerging wide areas of lower and fertile valleys, caused deforestation for the construction of linking roads. In this way the slightly better position of Himachal Pradesh in comparison to the national averages is fallacious. A little disturbance of forest cover in Himachal Pradesh creates havoc in hill areas by way of siltation, landslides and such other devastations. So it can be underlined that Himachal Pradesh needs a better understanding of the utility of forests with regard to the ecological balance of the State.

The forest policy of the State, the various schemes planned and undertaken, the financial provisions envisaged in various plans both by the State Government and by the Central Government, the cooperation envisaged the local populace for various schemes of social forestry by way of Joint Forest Management, and ambitions projections for the 10th Five Year Plan, and up to the turn of the century all indicate an awareness of the utility of forests not only as a big reservoir of economic resources, but also biggest single factor for the maintenance of ecological balance.

For hill states like Himachal Pradesh, where the forest has to protect hillsides against erosion, moderate the water flow and ameliorate physical and chemical factor of the locality, the National Forest policy lays down that forests should cover two-thirds of the geographical area. As per the legal definition of the term the forest cover should be 37,591 sq. kms. or 67.52 per cent of the total geographical area of Himachal Pradesh. But in reality as per the analysis the density is much less. Nearly 16,376 sq. kms. or 29.41 per cent of the so-called forest area is under alpine pastures and perpetual snow cover. This leaves only 21,215 sq. kms. i.e. 38.11 per cent of the geographical area under forest cover in Himachal Pradesh, whereas, as per the Himachal State Forest Policy, the required target to increase forest cover in Himachal Pradesh was 50 per cent of total geographical area by 2000 A.D.

It is observed that only 12,254 sq. kms. area falling into reserve forest and demarcated protected forest category has been demarcated on the ground and the rest of the area is yet to be demarcated with boundary pillars. Only 92.44 sq. kms (24.6%) of the forest area out of the total forest area stand entered into revenue record. This situation has created problem for forest protection.

The district-wise figures of forest cover in Himachal Pradesh reveals that some of the districts, particularly those of Chamba, Kullu, Mandi and Shimla are well forested, whereas other like Lahaul and Spiti, Kinnaur, Bilaspur have a low coverage of forest area.

With regard to plantation of fast growing species in the State to cover geographical area under forest, large scale plantations of different species raised in the State under various schemes and these cover an area of 30,000 ha. per year. Out of the total forest area of 37,591 sq. kms, almost all the accessible area with vegetative cover has been brought under working plans in the State.

The system of grant of timber (TD) to the right-holders at the concessional rates in Himachal Pradesh under the provision of Settlement Reports in various districts, misuse of TD rights has been observed. People in the State have been acquired T.D. Rights more as a routine phenomenon than to meet their actual needs. Present rates are completely obsolete as there is sharp increase in value of timber whereas rates fixed in the year 1873. It is however; laid down in the Settlement that exercise of rights is limited to the extent, beyond which a forest is unable to bear the same. Actually this is not being done and the capacity of a forest is being taxed beyond limits. A villager wants a tree of his choice, convenience and near to his place and marking officer just to oblige, ignores his profession; silviculture has thus become culture of mutual interest. Due to this malpractice, the forests near the villages and towns have been opened up very much and hardly any tree can be taken normally. The depletion and denudation of forests in the State resulting therein the ecological degradation and environmental hazards.

Joint Management of Forest (JFM) is a sharing of responsibilities, control, decision-making authority and products over forest lands between the Government and local users groups. The primary purpose of JFM in Himachal Pradesh is to ensure sustainability of forest resources of local level through improvements in forest condition and productivity. During project period, local people were involved in various forestry programmes, under various components of social forestry projects. If the Forest Department and the State Government really want to involve people in generating Himachal's forests, it has to change the very basic framework of JFM, in response to the field realities and the experience of the community forest management. The new framework would entail first recognizing the village forest committee as an independent entity and not an appendage of the department, which exists just to project. It has to be given the authority and autonomy to manage the forest. This means that the Forest Department will not be central to JFM as it is today but the people will be given the primary importance with decision-making powers. Ultimately, the Forest Department will have to play the role of an advisor and facilitator. That is the only way to save our forests.

Conservation strategies towards forest in the State like Himachal Pradesh need to be co-ordinated with all other interested groups including the stakeholders to seek solution to problems related to various linked issues. This means that various State government agencies need to work in concert to promote non-timber forest products and amenity value of forest resources. Joint Forest Management, which has a greater likelihood of success, needs to be promoted to form a forceful movement involving people for conservation and sustainable use of local forest resources in the State.

The problem of environmental conservation and development is quite complex and there is no single solution. Any viable strategy must take into account not only the physical nature of the problem but also the human factor involved. Moreover, mere legislation can never be a solution unless it is enforced strictly. If the Government of Himachal Pradesh truly concerned to save further degradation, there is an urgent need to implement environment protection laws efficiently, otherwise, the vast majority of the people of the State both in urban and rural area will continue to pay the price for misdeeds of recalcitrant few.

The Himachal Pradesh Environment Protection and Pollution Control Board is working within the ambit of the functions bestowed on it under Section 17 of the Water (Prevention and Control of Pollution) Act, 1974, and the Air (Prevention and Control of Pollution) Act, 1981 ensures sustainable development with due regard to the environment protection and conservation.

Although, the State Board is functioning to protect the Water and Air Pollution in the State, yet its functioning is not as satisfactory as it should have been. The State Pollution Control Board is basically an administrative agency having advisory powers. It has no direct legal duty to prosecute the defaulters. It has also no legal sanction to enforce its policies. In order to make State Pollution Control Board more effective to combat the environment pollution, the administrative bodies meant for the purpose must be institutionally, legally and financially strong enough to take effective steps and action to plan and manage the environmental problems. The Pollution Control Administrative Authorities must have independent powers to implement their decisions. Further, the Board under Water and Air Pollution Acts must pressurize the polluting units for the proper channelisation of polluting effluents.

The State Pollution Control Board is making strenuous efforts to tackle the problems of pollution in various ways in Himachal Pradesh by taking protecting measures of water, air pollution control system and number of samples of water and air have been conducted by the State Pollution Control Board.

Although, the State Pollution Control Board is working hard for effective implementation of Acts, the Board has not been empowered to enforce its policies and decision. Thus, the State Pollution Control Board is just acting as an advisory body to the State Government.

The Board feels helpless in taking action against industrialists on violation of law. The Board under Water Act has no powers to granting or not granting consent to discharge effluents. The Pollution Control Board is not getting cooperation from industries concerned. The industries hesitate to apply for grant of consent of the Board for installing anti-pollution treatment plants because it may cause financial and technological stress on them.

To make the State Pollution Control Board a potential agency it must be authorized to consult other agencies, which are dealing with the policies regarding the environmental conservation and development projects and programmes and other activities relating for the improvement of eco-system. It is suggested that the citizens much have the rights through Pollution Control Board, use the litigation process for the protection of air, water and natural resources and to participate more effectively in major government and corporated decision-making process.

Scientific and technological advancement and contribution is bearing an important role in future development, particularly of developing State like Himachal Pradesh. This will enshrine in future fulfilment of common man's basic minimum needs, self-reliance and ecological soundness by way of environment protection, conservation and development not only at the national level but also at grassroot level.

The objectives for which the State Council for Science, Technology and Environment, H.P., providing immense satisfaction by contributing significantly to the overall environmental protection and development in the State.

The State Council has introduced a number of technologies like Hand pumps, Solar Passive Housing Technology, Roof top rain-water harvesting, tapping the Solar Energy potential and Remote Sensing activities in the State. The Council is effectively implementing all these facilities available to preserve and develop the environmental related programmes and projects with the assistance of Central Government Departments like Department of Space, Ministry of Non-Conventional Energy Sources, Ministry of Environment and Forests and Department of Science and Technology.

Himachal Pradesh is the first State in the country to introduce Solar Passive Building Technology in the design and construction of government and semi-government buildings on large scale. The State Council for Science, Technology and Environment, H.P. has taken an important policy decision for implementation of Solar Passive Building Technology in the State and has achieved the goal by designing and constructing the various government and semi-government buildings. This is an important achievement of the State Council to save the conventional energy along with the pollution control.

Creating awareness amongst the public on the issues of environment is an another area where the State Council for Science,

Technology and Environment, H.P. has managed certain issues by taking initiatives under Solid Waste Management Programme Scheme, controlling the nuisance of polythene have been successfully brought in the forefront, on which policy and legislative measures have been initiated by the State Government. Similarly, conservation and management of Wetlands has been successfully completed to check the rate of siltation, plantation and socio-economic studies of the wet-lands. The roof top rainwater harvesting programme has also been made mandatory in urban area to conserve water and recharge ground water table. The Council is also effectively contributing in Bio-diversity Conservation and Monitoring in H.P. under AUSAID project for involving local people in diversity assessment and monitoring.

The Council has also been in the fore-front of the campaign for creating awareness about environmental issues by taking a number of initiatives by organising environmental awareness programmes and popularizing technological innovations through media.

Remote Sensing Technology has opened up new vistas for natural resources inventory monitoring. With the extension of the capability beyond the visible part of the electro magnetic spectrum, humankind now has access to information hitherto unknown to him. Himachal Pradesh Remote Sensing Cell, a wing of the State Council for Science, Technology and Environment, is utilizing various facilities, expertise available, data library in the State for hydrogeomorphological mapping, liniment mapping, generation of digital database of the wasteland, wetland inventory of the entire state and evaluation of natural resources.

The State Council has achieved the objective of saving the environment by utilizing consultancy services of Remote Sensing techniques in the field of groundwater development, Geo-technical investigation, pre-feasibility, Studies of Micro Hydel Projects, Environment Assessment Studies in the State by using Remote Sensing Satellite data.

In order to give more thrust to Integrated Rural Energy Planning Programme (IREP) and to institutionalized various programmes of non-conventional energy sources, which are suited for decentralized applications in the State HIMURJA is playing a vital role in the economic development along with environment conservation plans for the State. This Energy Development Agency concentrating in the State by providing non-conventional energy in rural areas in way of solar energy, solar water heating system, solar cookers and PV lights. By providing all these facilities in rural areas, HIMURJA is achieving the objective of the Agency by reducing the conventional energy consumption and maintaining the environmental and ecological balance and quality of life has also been improved.

The main objectives for which the Agency is concentrating relating to implementation and promotion of Non-Conventional Energy Sources throughout the State and to construct Micro Hydel Programmes upto 3 MW capacities through private investment in the State.

In analyzing the Solar Thermal Extension Programme it has been observed that the Government of Himachal Pradesh has taken a effective decision to make the installation of Solar Water Heating Systems mandatory in all government buildings and institutions in the State, which is a healthy step to save the energy in the State particularly in the temperate and cold regions. Thus, Himachal Pradesh is the first State in the country to make this technology compulsory and this step has been widely acclaimed.

Though hundred per cent electrification has been achieved in Himachal Pradesh, yet there are a number of hamlets and pockets of houses which are still unelectrified, some of these houses are so remotely located that the people living there cannot have hope for electrification by conventional means since it was not possible to lay the distribution lines for covering these areas as it was very costly proposition. Keeping in view, the above hurdles in those remote areas, HIMURJA, is the Agency which is providing Solar Photovoltaic Systems for these identified remote locations in the State by providing Solar PV Lights, domestic PV lights and by distributing PV lanterns at subsidized rates in different IREP, Blocks.

Energy conservation programme is another important area where HIMURJA is providing energy efficient devices like Nutan Stoves and Nutan Jyoti, etc. to identified IRDP families in the selected IREP Blocks for saving the energy sources by utilizing these energy saving devices. The results have shown marginal achievements in the high altitude with increase thermal efficiency of 45 per cent.

Similarly, with regard to Small Hydro Power Generation up to 3 MW, the State of Himachal Pradesh has a vast potential of about 20,000 MW out of which 4400 MW has been harnessed so far. There is an estimated potential of approximately 750 MW in the Small Hydro Power (SHP) Sector i.e. less than 3 MW. Out of this potential, approximately 600 MW at 431 sites with capacities ranging from 3 KW to 100 KW has so far been identified. The HIMURJA for achieving this purpose along with the MPP Power Department has made a progress to implement agreements and the power purchase agreements signed for 20 projects with potential of 45.95 MW capacity in the first phase of private sector participation. In the second phase, 24 projects having an aggregate capacity of 50.24 MW has been signed.

HIMURJA has also framed proposals with the collaboration of World Bank under UNDP-GEF (Global Environment Facility) Hilly Hydro Projects, which aims to achieve reduction in global warming, protection of bio-diversity in the Himalayan and Sub-Himalayan regions. The UNDP-GEF India Hilly Hydro Project is the first project from India to be included in the Global Environment Facility (GEF) portfolio. HIMURJA is contributing as a developer in these projects with having capacity ranging between 100 KW to 400 KW of capacity for the execution of the projects which highlights the aims and objectives of the Agency to promote, popularize and provide appropriate energy at affordable prices and also encourage R&D efforts in the renewal energy sector in the State.

The problem of environment conservation and development has in recent times engaged the attention of various organisations, agencies and institutions. An introduction of large amounts of pollutants causes serious problems for the life on the earth. Because of these constraints, environmental conservation and development—An Analysis of Administrative Structure and Policy Issues adopted by the Himachal State Government are essential for maintaining the ecological balance in the State. The Government of Himachal Pradesh to achieve this purpose is running certain organisations and agencies to ensure environmental conservation and development structure along with implementing machinery to achieve the desired goals in the State with the assistance of organisations like Department of Forest, H.P. State Environment Protection and Pollution Control Board, State Council for Science, Technology and Environment, H.P. and HIMURJA (H.P. Government Energy Development Agency).

It is observed that though there are various organisations and agencies of the State Government which are engaged in implementation of environmental conservation and developmental policies. There is a lack of co-ordination between these organisations and agencies of the State Government. It is generally observed that these organisations and agencies are functioning in the State only as advisory bodies, in nature, to the State Government. It is also observed that these agencies are lacking in policy implementation due to lack of financial resources, legislative measures, administrative will, lack of people's participation, environmental education among the general masses, autonomy and judicial approach to environmental law in the State.

It is in the interest of the State Government that while framing and implementing the various policies to protect the environment in the State, these organisations and agencies should be given sufficient power to take a direct action against the defaulters.

The government should give a highest priority to save and solve the problem of environment conservation in the State with the assistance of an integrated approach to various organisations and agencies of the State Government.

There is an urgent need for the Environment Protection Administration that it should be free from politics to allow impartial implementation of environmental laws.

Outright grant-in-aid is not a sound method of financing public agencies, such as HIMURJA, Council for Science, Technology and Environment, H.P. and State Pollution Control Board. It makes the organisations lax, extravagant and wasteful under these dispensation. These agencies should be based on sound commercial ground. There should be sound provisions for financial resource generation to fight with the problems in an effective and efficient manner.

Social awareness to environmental education can help in isolating those who are polluting the environment. For this purpose, private and public agencies must join hands and make people aware of their environment and problems effecting it. Educational institutions can also play an important role in arousing civic consciousness for abatement of environmental pollution by ensuring that every citizen knows enough about the environment to take an intelligent interest in pollution problems. For this, environmental education should be made an essential part of curriculum by the State Government in all schools and colleges.

To sum up, environmental problems in the country has raised tremendous dimensions and if needed steps are not taken to meet this challenge and to contain their crisis, there will be further environmental deterioration having deep effects on human life and other species. There is a need to have a national thinking without bias and partial considerations. If this is not done and policies and programme are not framed, executed, accessed and monitored without dedication and devotion, the problem of environmental degradation well definitely be miserable to the life of masses. Thus, Himachal Pradesh has a greater constraints to face greater responsibilities to shoulders to maintain a better eco-system in the State and its resultant benefits for the State in particular and Nation in general.

Notes and References

1. Neela Mukherjee (1997), "Forests, Indigenous Committees and Sustainable Development", *Kurukshetra (*January-February, p. 13.
2. Edmunds and John Letey (1973), *Environmental Administration*, New York: McGraw-Hill, p. 3.
3. Edmunds and John Letey (1973) *Environmental Administration*, McGraw Book Company, New York, pp. 15-16.
4. *Ibid.*, p. 3.
5. Ahmed Fahinuddin in his article, "Environmental Management," (1987), published in the book, *Environmental Education for Conservation and Development,* edited by Desh Bandhu and G. Berberet, Natraj Publishers, Dehradun, p. 343,
6. Edmunds and Letey (1973), *op. cit.*, pp. 20, 21.
7. A.B. Garlauskas (1975), "Conceptual Framework of Environmental Management", *Journal of Environment*, 3: 185-203.
8. Charter—Principal-1.
9. Principle 12.
10. National Committee on Environment Planning and Co-ordination, 1972.
11. Attar Chand (1980), *Environmental Challengs: A Global Survey*, UDH Publishers, New Delhi, p. 64.
12. It has been estimated that there are more than 200 Central or State enactment which have a direct or indirect relation with environmental protection, see, Inaugural Address by J.K. Kaushal former Minister of Law, at the National Seminar on 'Law Towards Environmental Protection, held at Chandigarh (1984).
13. Section 3(2) of the Act.

14. Tiwari Committee Report, Supra note 9, p. 1924.
15. Fourth Five-Year Plan (1969-74), p. 46 (Para II).
16 Suresh Jain (1985), (ed.), Environmental Laws in India, p. 592; Sixth Five Year Plan (1980-85), p. 343.
17. Seventh Five Year Plan, Vol. II, Chapter 18, Government of India Publication, New Delhi, pp. 385-94.
18. R.K. Sapru (ed.), (1987), *Forest, Environment and Development*, Ashish Publishing House, Delhi, p.181.
19. T.N. Khoshoo (1986), Environmental Priorities in India and Sustainable Development. Presidential Address, 73rd Session Indian Science Congress. Association, New Delhi, p. 221.
20. F. Warner (1982), Indo-Swedish Forestry Programme II. 1982-83 to 1986-87. Background document. Swedish Embassy, Development Corporation Office, New Delhi, pp. 1-92.
21. *Op. cit.*, p. 221.
22. S.D. Thapar (1974), Forestry in the Year 2001. Ford Foundation, New Delhi.
23. *Ibid.*
24. M. Gadgil and R. Guha (1992), *This Fissured Land*, Oxford University Press, New Delhi.
25. R. Guha (1983) "Forestry in British and Post-British India: A Historical Analysis". *Economical and Political Weekly*, Bombay. 29 October and 5 November.
26. A Kothari, P. Pandey, S. Singh and D. Vanava (1989) : Management of National Parks and Santuaries in India: A Status Report/11PA, New Delhi.
27. *Hindustan Times*, December 3, 1986, New Delhi.
28. D.K. Pandey (1997), "Forest Policy and Management in India", *Kurukhetra*, Jan.-Feb., Delhi, p. 61.
29. *Ibid.*, p. 61.
30. H. South Wick Charles (1972), *Ecology and the Quality of our Environment*. D.Van Nestrand Company, New York, p. Overview XII.
31. Fain C. Theodore (1967) *Ecological System and the Environment*, p. 7.
32. Fain C. Theodore (1976), *ibid.*, p.37.
33. H.S. Stephan and V.B. Burton (1973), *Forest Ecology*, The Ronand Press Company, New Delhi, p. 1.
34. J. Bandyopadhyay, N.D. Jayal, U. Schoetti and Chhatarpati (ed.) (1985), *India's Environment: Crises and Responses, Crises*

in Forest Resource Management, Natraj Publishers, Dehradun, p. 7.

35. Charles J. Taylor (1962), *Tropical Forestry*, Oxford University Press, New York, Tronto, pp. 1-19.
36. *Ibid.*
37. National Forest Policy (1988), Minstry of Environment and Forests.
38. Charles J. Taylor (1962), *Tropical Forestry*, Oxford University Press, New York, Toronto, pp. 1-19.
39. A Citizen's Report (1982), The State of India's Environment, Centre for Science and Environment, New Delhi, p. 33.
40. J. Bandyopadhyay, N.D. Jayal, and Chhatrapati Singh (ed.) (1985), *Ibid.*, p. 7.
41. *Ibid.*, p. 7.
42. *Ibid.*, p. 8.
43. *Ibid.*, p. 8.
44. *Ibid.*, p. 8.
45. Development Profile of Himachal Pradesh (1985). Directorate of Economic and Statistics, Government of Himachal Pradesh.
46. Forest Department Record.
47. State of The Environment Report—Himachal Pradesh.
48. Government of Himachal Pradesh, Draft Annual Plan (1986-87) Planning Department, Shimla, p. 81.
49. S.S. Negi, IWDP (Hills), Himachal Pradesh, Workshop on Formulation of New Community Based, August 1998, Department of Forest, H.P. Shimla.
50. H.P. Forest Sector Review—Main Report, June 2000.
51. Annual Report, HPCB, 1997-98.
52. Annual Reports, HPCB.
53. Jermer, M.K. 1987, *Water Resources and Water Management*, Elsevier, Amsterdam.
54. Zoning Atlas for Sitting of Industries (1997), based on Environmental Conservations, Solan District, Himachal Pradesh, Centre Pollution Control Board and Himachal Pradesh State Pollution Control Board.
55. Memorandum of Association, State Council for Science, Technology and Environment, Himachal Pradesh.
56. See Organizational Chart of State Council for Science, Technology and Environment, Himachal Pradesh.
57. *Alternatives*, Quarterly Newsletter of the State Council,

Vol. VI, April-June, 1999.

58. *Alternatives*, Quarterly Newsletter of the State Council for Science, Technology and Evnirnment, H.P., Vol. VI, April-June, 1999.
59. Brief Report on the Activities, State Council for Science, Technology and Environment, Shimla.
60. Brief Report on the Activities, State Council for Science, Technology and Environment, Shimla.
61. Annual Action Plan, 1998-99, State Council for Science, Technology and Environment, H.P.
62. Brief Report on the Activities, State Council for Science, Technology and Environment, H.P.
63. N.K. Shastree (1997), *Environment Resource Management*, Anmol Publications, New Delhi.
64. N.K. Uberoi (1999), *Environment Management*, Excel Books, New Delhi, p. 3.

Bibliography

Books

Agarwal, V.P. and S.V.S. Rana. *Science Development and Environment.* Musafarnagar: Society of Biosciences, 1987.

Ahamad, Yusuf, J. (ed.) *Environment Decision-Making; An Introduction to the Application of Cost-benefit Analysis.* London: Holder and Stoughton, 1983.

A. Salem, Fassals. *Economical Dimensions of Development Administration.* New York: International Book Distribution, 1977.

Anderson, Frederick R. and others. *Environmental Improvement Through Economic Incentives;* Baltimore: John Hopkins, 1978.

Andrews, Suzanna and Others (ed.). *The World Environment Handbook: A Directory of Government Natural Resource Management Agencies in 144 Countries.* New York: World Environment Centre, 1982.

Baden, John and Ricarhd L. Stroup (eds.) *Bureaucracy vs. Environment: The Environmental Cost of Bureaucratic Governance.* Ann Arbor: University of Michigan Press, 1981.

Banerjee, Brojendra Nath. *Environmental Pollution and Bhopal Killings.* Delhi: Gian, 1987.

Barrett, Richard, N. (ed.). *International Dimensions of the Environmental Crises.* Boulder: West View, 1982.

Bartelmus, Peter. *Environment and Development.* London: Allen and Unwin,1986.

Baumol, William, J. and Wallance, E. Oates. *The Theory of Environmental Policy.* Cambridge: Cambridge University Press, 1988.

Beale, Jack, G. *The Manager and Environment: General Theory and Practice of Environmental Management.* New York: Pergamon, 1980.

Bhargava, Gopal. *Environmental Pollution and Law.* Bombay: Commerce Pamphlets, 1981.

Bhatt, S. *Environmental Laws and Water Resources Management.* New Delhi: Radiant, 1986.

Bielenstein, Dieter (ed.). *One World Only Industrialization and Environment.* Tokyo: Friedrich-Ebert-Stiftung, 1974.

Brown, Standford M. and Theodore R. Forrest, Jr. *Environmental Health Law.* New York: Praeger, 1984.

Caldwell, Lynton K. *International Environmental Policy: Emergence and Dimensions.* Duke: Duke Press, 1984.

Caldwell, Lynton K. *Man and His Environment: Policy and Administration.* New York: Harper and Row, 1975..

Clark, B.D. and others. *Environmental Impact Assessment: A Bibliography with Abstracts.* London: Mansell, 1980.

Desh Bandhu and G. Barberet (ed.) *Environmental Education for Conservation and Development: Proceedings of the Second International Conference on Environmental Education.* New Delhi: Indian Environmental Society, 1987.

Desh Bandhu (ed.). *Environmental Management.* (Selected Papers at Seminar held at Indian National Science Academy, New Delhi during June 5-7, 1980. New Delhi: Indian Environmental Society, 1981.

Desh Bandhu and others (ed.). *Managing the Environment Proceedings of College, Darjeeling, Seva Mandir, Udaipur, Indian National Science Academy.* New Delhi during March-April 1978, Delhi: Indian Environment Society, 1978.

Diwan, Paras (ed.). *Environment Protection: Problems, Policy Administration.* New Delhi: Deep and Deep, 1987.

Ehrich, Paul R. and others. *Human Ecology: Problems and Solutions.* New York: WH Freeman, 1973.

Etherington, John R. *Environment and Plan Ecology.* New Delhi: Wiley Eastern, 1976.

Grad, Frank P. and others. *Environmental Control: Priorities, Policies and the Law.* New York: Columbia University, 1971.

Henning, Daniel H. *Environmental Policy and Administration.* New York: American Elsevier, 1974.

Indian Institute of Public Administration, New Delhi. *Environmental Policy in India.* Edited by Shekhar Singh, New Delhi: The Institute, 1984.

Indian Institute of Public Administration. *Environmental Studied Division Management of National Parks and Sanctuaries in India: A Status Report,* by Ashish Kothari, and Others, New Delhi, Environmental Studies Division. IIPA. 1989.

Jain, Suresh and Vimla Jain. *Environment Planning and Control.* Brookfield: Grower, 1982.

Katyal, T. and Satake. *Environmental Pollution.* New Delhi: Anmol, 1989.

Khoshoo, T.N. *Environmental Concerns and Strategies.* New Delhi: Times Press, 1984.

Malviya, R.A. *Environmental Pollution and Its Control Under International Law.* Allahabad: Chugh, 1987.

Mann, Dean E. (ed.) *Environmental Policy Formation: The Impact of Values, Ideology and Standards.* Lexington: Lexington, 1981.

Mohan, I. *Environment and Habitant.* New Delhi: Ashish, 1989.

Mohan, I. *Environmental Awareness and Urban Development.* New Delhi: Ashish, 1988.

Murphy, Earl Finbar. *Man and His Environment: Law.* New York: Harper and Row, 1971.

Nijkamp, Peter. *Environmental Policy Analysis: Operational Methods and Models.* Chichester: John Wiley, 1980.

Pal, B.P. *Environmental Conservation and Development.* Dehradun: Natraj, 1982.

Rama Rao, R. *Environmental Problems of Development and Developing Countries.* New Delhi: Economic and Scientific Research Foundation, 1976.

Roster, Bernd and other (ed.) *International Protection of the Environment Management in India.* New Delhi: Ashish, 1987.

Singh, S. *Principles of Environmental Conservation.* Dehradun: ID, 1989.

Singh, Pramod. *Environmental Pollution and Management.* Allahabad: Chugh, 1985.

Singh, Ram Bali. *Studies in Environment and Development.* New Delhi: Commonwealth, 1988.

Vijaybhushan. *Environmental Planning and Its Implementation.* New Delhi: 11PA, 1980. (APPPA Thesis 1979-80).

Articles

Baskar, H. "Environmental Planning, Protection, Preservation and Perpetuation. *The Administrator,* 31:3 (July-September 1986).

Basu, N.G. "Ecology and Development," *Mainstream,* 27 (40) 2 Jul. 89.

Bates, Gerry. "Environmental Impact Assessment: The Australian Experience. *Journal of Planning and Environment* Law, (November 1979).

Bawa, Vijay S. "On Optimal Pollution Control Policies:" *Management Science* (Application Series) 21:12 (August 1975).

Boojh Ram. "Conservation of Environment." *Civil Affairs,* 35:11 (June 1988).

Boschken, Hrrman L. "The Demands of Conflicting Change on Public

Enterprise: West Coast Seaport Development and Environmental Regulation." *Public Administration Review*, 42 (May-June 1982)

Chandrasekahran, N.S. "Environmental Protection: Two Steps Forward, One Step Back." *Journal of the Indian Law Institute,* 30:2 (April-June 1988).

Duinker, Peter N. and Gordon L. Baskerville. "A Systematic Approach to Forecasting in Environmental Impact Assessment." *Journal of Environmental Management* 23:3 (October 1986).

Dwivedi, O.P. and B. Kishore. "Protecting the Environment from Pollution: A Review of India's Legal and Institutional Mechanism." *Asian Survey*, 22:9 (September 1982).

Hadden, Susan G. "Statues and Standards for Pollution Control in India." *Economic and Political Weekly,* 22:16 (18 April 1987).

Jain, Suresh. "Environmental Law in India." *Indian Journal of Public Administration*," 31:2 (April-June 1985).

Lonergan, S.C. and G. Corklin. "The Use of Input-Output Analysis in Environmental Planning." *Journal of Environmental Management,* 20:2 (March 1985).

Lorrain-Smith, Roy. "The Nature of Environmental Management." *Journal of Environmental Management,* 14:3 (April 1982).

Sethi, Narendra K. "Environmental Management." *Economic Times,* (3 May 1977).

Sethi, Om Parkash. "Good Environment: Development Versus Environment." *Young India*, 1A: 7 (19 May 1989).

Periodicals and Reports

Alternatives, Quarterly Newsletter of the Council for Science, Technology and Environment, H.P.

Annual Administrative Reports, Forest Department, State Council for Science, Technology and Environment, H.P., H.P. Pollution Control Board and HIMURJA (An Energy Development Agency) Government of H.P.

Bio Energy News, A Quarterly Newsletter of the National Bio-Energy Board (MONES) GOI.

Brief Report on the Activities, State Council for Science, Technology and Environment, Shimla.

Brief Note on the Activities of HIMURJA.

Brief Facts Himachal Pradesh 2000, Department of Economics and Statistics, H.P.

Convention of Forest Officers, April 27-28, 1994, Department of Forest, H.P.

Economic Survey 2001, Himachal Pradesh, Department of Economics and Statistics.

Guidelines for Entrepreneurs on Environmental Related Clearances H.P. State Pollution Control Board, Hotel King's, The Mall, Shimla-171001.

Himachal Forests 1989, Forest Department, H.P.

H.P. Forest Statistics 1996, Forest Department, H.P.

Himachal Pradesh Forest Sector Review, Main Report, June 2000.

Himachal Forest 1999, Forest Department, H.P.

Himachal in Figures 2000, Department of Economics and Statistics, Government of H.P.

Millennium Special 2000—Renewable Energy, Energy Efficiency Financing Guidelines, IREDA.

Paryavaran Abstracts, Department of Environments, GOI, New Delhi.

Solar Passive Housing Design Guidelines for Cold Climates, State Council for Science, Technology and Environment, H.P.

Workshop on Formulation of New Community Based People Oriented Afforestation Scheme on August, 1998, H.P. Forest Department.

Zoning Atlas for Setting of Industries (based on Environment consideration), Solan District (HP), Central Pollution Control Board, HPCB, November, 1977.

Index